WRITING WITH REASON
Logic for Composition

WRITING WITH REASON
Logic for Composition

MONROE C. BEARDSLEY

Temple University

PRENTICE-HALL, INC., ENGLEWOOD CLIFFS, NEW JERSEY

Library of Congress Cataloging in Publication Data

BEARDSLEY, MONROE C
  Writing with reason.

  Includes index.
  1. Exposition (Rhetoric) 2. Logic. I. Title.
PE1429.B4   808   75-31837
ISBN 0-13-970301-2 pbk.

© 1976 by PRENTICE-HALL, INC.
Englewood Cliffs, New Jersey

Printed in the United States of America

10   9   8   7   6   5   4   3   2   1

PRENTICE-HALL INTERNATIONAL, INC., *London*
PRENTICE-HALL OF AUSTRALIA, PTY. LTD., *Sydney*
PRENTICE-HALL OF CANADA, LTD., *Toronto*
PRENTICE-HALL OF INDIA PRIVATE LIMITED, *New Delhi*
PRENTICE-HALL OF JAPAN, INC., *Tokyo*
PRENTICE-HALL OF SOUTHEAST ASIA (PTE.) LTD., *Singapore*

CONTENTS

PREFACE

This book is about writing—more particularly, about the indispensable role of logic in good writing. It is not about imaginative writing, which creates fiction, poetry, and drama, but about discursive writing, which aims primarily to influence belief—that is, to inform (or sometimes misinform), to convince, to enlighten, to produce new understanding or insight.

In this book, pieces of discursive writing are called "compositions." This term is a handy label for writings of many sorts: an editorial, a news story, a book review, a magazine article, a history of the American Revolution. The following letter is, for example, a composition:

To the Editor:
    For consideration by those legislators who advocate the enactment of laws designed to deny responsible persons the right to possess self-protecting firearms, may I, through the courtesy of your newspaper, pose this simple question:

How do such lawmakers reconcile their position with the fact that the United States Government has used untold billions of tax dollars to buy and distribute firearms to foreign nations, to the end that their peoples might defend themselves against aggression?

I suggest that if and when law-enforcement agencies and our judiciary find themselves capable of protecting our lives and property rights, the fear and hysteria about guns and their control will, like old soldiers, just fade away. (*The New York Times*, April 16, 1975)*

A good composition, we recognize, must be coherent. What, then, does coherence depend upon? In his first paragraph, this writer announces that he is opposed to laws that prohibit "responsible persons" from possessing guns. In the second paragraph he argues, in effect, that such laws are inconsistent with the nation's policy of supplying armaments to other nations. Do these two paragraphs fit together coherently? That depends on whether the logical connection which the writer thinks he sees is a genuine one. If gun-control laws and international armament arrangements are logically connected (if the same general principles apply to both), the letter is coherent; if they are not, it falls apart. Logic makes the difference.

A good composition, we also recognize, is clear; we can grasp what it is saying, and why. Is this letter clear? The question is one of interpretation. Do you understand what "self-protecting firearms" are, and how they differ from firearms that are *not* "self-protecting"? Are rockets and bombing planes which the United States supplies to other nations "firearms" in the same sense as a Smith and Wesson .38? Perhaps you will decide that the writer has indeed made these points clear. If not, you have to conclude that he has not thought out his own position very well, has only a vague idea of what he is arguing for or against, and may even have an inconsistent view. These faults are matters of logic.

A good composition, we also recognize, is free from faults of style; it moves without awkwardness or jarring from phrase to phrase, from sentence to sentence. But even faults of style are sometimes logical faults. When this writer compares fear and hysteria with old soldiers, in that both "just fade away," do you find the comparison rather odd? Are the old soldiers dragged in as a mere cliché? The answer depends on how relevant they are—and relevance is a matter of logic.

It would be a considerable oversimplification to say that good thinking is the secret of good writing, or that poor writing is always due to poor thinking. But writing and thinking are intimately connected, and what helps us to think better will also help us to write better.

Although logic is a large subject, there is a limited set of its prin-

*© 1975 by The New York Times Company. Reprinted by permission.

ciples that can be studied by themselves and put to good use in a great deal of writing. This small book presents such principles; it offers the rudiments of logic that are most useful to the student of composition. They are principles of good reasoning: it is by following them that writers produce those occasional reports or editorials that strike us by the force, clarity, and cogency of their arguments. They are also principles that enable us to identify poor reasoning: it is when they are violated that we get, for example, Snoopy's reasoning in the *Peanuts* cartoon:

© *1975 United Feature Syndicate, Inc.*

Snoopy has his own explanation. What's funny about it? (See Chapter 12.)

You cannot expect to attain ease in wielding the concepts and principles of logic merely by abstract study. You will have to put them to work, in analyzing what others have written, to see where they go wrong, and in your own writing, to make sure that you go right. So the exercises in this book, which turn up frequently, are of both sorts. They present material to examine and criticize logically, and they propose projects for writing.

As a preparation for doing these exercises, the text includes many examples of both poor reasoning and good reasoning. Here and there I have pointed up this contrast by marking the logically acceptable passages with a " ✓ " and the offending passages with an "X".

I should like to thank William H. Oliver and Wayne Spohr of Prentice-Hall for proposing this book and for their excellent advice and warm encouragement along the way. I owe many improvements in the text to several composition teachers who read all or part of this book in manuscript and were generous in their suggestions: Robert Bain, University of North Carolina; Vincent Gillespie, Kansas State University; George D. Haich, Georgia State University; Stephen Reid, Colorado State University; and most especially Kevin Kerrane, University of Delaware. And I am most grateful to Mrs. Grace Stuart for her enormous help in preparing the manuscript for the press.

M.C.B.

WRITING WITH REASON

Logic for Composition

1

WOULD YOU BELIEVE?

inference and argument

You're looking down at a cement sidewalk, and two thoughts occur to you: (1) there is a small footprint in the sidewalk; (2) a child stepped into it before the cement hardened. No very unusual occurrence, to be sure. But there is an important difference between these two thoughts. You *see* the footprint; that is visibly here now. But you don't see the child stepping into the cement; that happened perhaps months ago, long before you got here. But you think: "A child stepped in" *because* you think: "There is a footprint." Whenever you think one thought *because* you think another thought, you are making an *inference*. You *see* the footprint; you *infer* the child. Inference is a transferral of belief from one idea to another.

This distinction is very basic. It is a familiar feature of our mental life. Many inferences, like the footprint inference, begin with something that is directly presented to you—a color, a smell, a sound, a taste:

> You hear the siren. You infer that a police car is coming.
> You smell gas in the kitchen. You infer that the stove's pilot light has gone out.
> You have a sour taste while drinking the milk. You infer that the milk is sour.

Other inferences begin with beliefs that you have already arrived at through previous inferences. The new inference takes you one step further:

> You believe that this building is the post office. You infer that you will be able to buy stamps inside.
> You believe that the mayor's political support is growing weaker. You infer that he will not run for office next time.
> You believe that your neighbor is a policeman. You infer that he carries a gun when he is off duty.
> You believe your neighbor carries a gun. You infer that he is a policeman.

In all these cases there are two ideas (these are the very simplest cases of inference, of course). One is the *basis* of the inference: what you infer *from*. The other is the *result* of the inference: what you infer *to*. They have to be distinct, or the inference goes nowhere, and is not a genuine inference at all. (If you already know that Independence Hall is on Chestnut Street, you can't infer that it is.) And they have to be connected, or the inference doesn't carry through. Consider these silly examples:

> You see dark clouds. You infer that the stock market went up six points last week.
> You hear the siren. You infer that mushroom soup is more popular than onion soup.
> You believe that this building is the post office. You infer that this is a good place to buy socks.

Why would nobody make such inferences as these? Because we can find no link between the supposed basis and the supposed result. In each of the earlier examples you saw a link—that is, another idea connecting the basis with the result. I didn't have to state them, but I could have. For example (italicizing the connecting idea):

> You hear the siren. *You know that sirens are used on police cars.* You infer that a police car is coming.
> You believe that this building is the post office. *You know that post*

offices sell stamps (when they are open). You believe that the post office is open. You infer that you will be able to buy stamps inside.

Perhaps the links you supplied were a little different from mine. Still, you must have found some link or you wouldn't have accepted my examples as natural ones. But what can we do with the silly examples?

You hear the siren. (   ) You infer that mushroom soup is more popular than onion soup.

There doesn't seem to be anything we could sensibly insert between these parentheses. Of course, you can imagine a possible connection: maybe the makers of mushroom soup are celebrating their victory over the onion-soup makers; or maybe the police are rushing to investigate the hijacking of a truckload of that popular mushroom soup. But you don't really know these things to be true, and you don't even believe them. So you can't use them as links in an inference.

You can't always tell for sure whether or not someone is making an inference—especially if the jump from the basis to the result seems a very wild or risky one. Certain key words often signal that an inference is taking place:

Inference Markers	
since	therefore
because	so
for	hence
	thus
	consequently

Let us call these words, and their numerous approximate synonyms, "inference markers."

He must be wise, *for* he has lived a long time.
He has lived a long time. *Consequently*, he must be wise.

Here the same inference is stated in two ways. The inference proceeds from "He has lived a long time" (the basis) to "He is wise" (the result). When inference markers are missing, we can still tell that an inference is being made if we see a possible connection that might plausibly lead someone to think one idea because he thinks the other:

Susan is sleepy. Susan is yawning.

You have to picture a likely situation. You might see Susan yawning, and you could be led to think that Susan must be sleepy. So there is probably an inference here: it moves from "Susan is yawning" (the basis of the inference) to "Susan is sleepy" (the result of the inference).

It is possible to write a composition that doesn't contain any inferences. But it would be quite unusual, and probably dull. Plain description is not inference, but most descriptions contain at least a hint of some of the inferences that led to the ideas being set forth and of some inferences that might legitimately be drawn from those ideas. Try describing a tree or the last few minutes of a basketball game without saying how you came to know or believe any of the things you say and without making any judgment about the implications of what you say.

Many compositions are concerned mainly with inference; they have extended inferences, involving perhaps many steps and many links, as their central structure. Their coherence, therefore, depends vitally on the writer's ability and willingness to make clear the basis and result of each inference, and also (even if he doesn't state them explicitly) the links that make the inferences understandable and sensible.

EXERCISE 1A

Which of the following are probably inferences? (Ask yourself: Could one of the ideas be plausibly inferred from the other?)

1. Susan is sleepy. She is also hungry.

2. Jonathan is coughing. Jonathan has a cold.

3. The parked car has a dent in it. Somebody bumped into it.

4. The car has a scratch on it. The car is a Buick.

5. Traffic is moving very slowly. There is a bottleneck up ahead.

6. Something should be done to improve the highway system around here. Traffic is moving very slowly.

7. The price of milk has gone up again. The price of butter is going down.

8. The Flyers' goalie has gone to the hospital. The Flyers will lose more games.

9. DDT is a danger to the environment. The hazards of oil spills have been reduced.

10. Mercy killing is illegal. Mercy killing is a violation of the patient's right to life.

When we say that a couple of people have gotten into an argument with each other, we mean (and it would be more exact to say) that they are in *dispute*. In a dispute the two parties disagree—that is, their beliefs are opposed in some way. And, as long as they don't come to blows, each of them *argues for* his position and against the other's. To argue is to attempt (by using spoken or written words) to change someone's mind by getting him to make an inference.

Arguing, then, involves three essential elements: (1) an assertion of what is to be established as the result of the inference ("Capital punishment is wrong")—this assertion is the *conclusion* of the argument; (2) an assertion of what is to be granted as a basis of the inference ("Capital punishment is cruel")—this assertion is a *reason* offered in support of the conclusion; it is a *premise* of the argument; (3) an inference marker or some substitute indication that an inference is to be made from the reason to the conclusion. The basic form of an argument, then, is:

(Reason)
Therefore: (Conclusion)

Or, to give another example:

If the government introduces price controls, the supply of food will decrease. (Reason)
Therefore: The government should not introduce price controls. (Conclusion)

This may not be a *great* argument, or even a good one, but never mind that for the moment.

No argument can be simpler than this one, which has one reason and one conclusion. Very many arguments are more complicated. Always, however, the basic pattern is the same, and to come to grips with an argument, no matter how complicated, you must distinguish the reasons from the conclusions—even when the same assertion plays both roles:

> When prices go down, food producers reduce production.
> *Therefore:* If the government introduces price controls, the supply of
>   food will decrease.
> *Therefore:* The government should not introduce price controls.

The second assertion here is a conclusion for which the first one is (offered as) a reason; the second is also (offered as) a reason for the third. So both the second and third assertions are conclusions in this argument, though they are supported by different reasons.

The term "reason" has two main meanings; we shall stick to one of them for the present. One can give a *reason why* something has happened (Why does the roof leak?) or why someone has done something (Why did Benedict Arnold decide to betray West Point?). That sort of reason is an *explanation* (see Chapter 12). In this chapter we are concerned with *reasons for believing*. A reason for believing that the government should not introduce price controls is that if price controls were introduced, the supply of food would decrease—assuming that the reason given is in fact true. For unless it is true that price controls diminish the supply of price-controlled goods, this assertion cannot be a reason for anything.

Unlike an explanation or a description or a narration, an argument does not merely state something. It nudges us toward an inference and guides the inference in the direction in which it is to go. And this is as important to keep in mind when constructing your own arguments as it is when considering the arguments of others. You must let your reader, or listener, know just what inference you want him to make, and why it is reasonable for him to make it.

This means that in setting forth an argument, your task is to make its structure, however complicated, as clear as possible. Your reader must be able to tell which are your reasons and which are your conclusions, and which reasons go with which conclusions. You are free to choose the order in which you develop the argument: you might put the conclusion first or the reason first. You are free to choose the inference markers that are most appropriate for the context, or to leave out inference markers if the context makes the situation clear. But you should give order to your argument, and you should make that order as plain as possible.

There are two general rules of order for argument construction. Neither is absolute, and sometimes they conflict and have to be mutually adjusted. Still, they are fundamental. First, as far as possible, group reasons for the same conclusion together, and keep them close to the conclusion they are to support. This is the Rule of Grouping. If reasons are scattered, it may be hard to discern their common role in the argument; and if they are separated from the relevant conclusion, the reader may not notice that they are reasons at all or may not grasp the point of introducing them. Second, as far as possible, keep the argument moving in one direction. This is the Rule of Direction. You may present some reasons that lead to a conclusion, and a further conclusion from that conclusion, and so on. Or you may begin by presenting your final conclusion, and work backwards to the reasons that support it, and the reasons behind those reasons, and so forth. But if you zigzag, the reader may easily get lost and begin to wonder where the argument is going and whether you understand it yourself. You are—or should be—the one in control.

Both rules are violated in this passage:

(1) It would be a mistake to abolish all laws that differentiate between men and women, since (2) women need special protection against various forms of exploitation. Hence, (3) the equal rights amendment should be defeated. It is also obvious that (4) women should not have to fight in wars. And, of course, (5) in divorce cases, the child should go with the mother, unless the court finds her incompetent or undesirable.

There seem to be five assertions here, which I have numbered for reference. Assertion 2 seems to be a reason for assertion 1, and 1 for 3. We may represent this relationship by a diagram, in which arrows stand for "therefore," or "is a reason for."

$$2 \searrow$$
$$1$$
$$\searrow 3$$

The argument would surely be clearer if these assertions were put in order according to the Rule of Direction: either 2, 1, 3 or 3, 1, 2. It is hard to be sure whether 4 is a reason for 1 or for 3—but 3 seems the more likely candidate. Although 4 follows immediately after 3, which is appropriate, it is separated from 1, the other reason for 3; so the argument would be still clearer if 1 and 4 were grouped together, according to the Rule of Grouping. Assertion 5 seems to be a reason for assertion 1, though it is widely separated from it; it ought to be grouped with 2. The whole argument can be diagramed as follows:

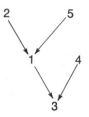

It is not always possible to live up to both rules completely when the argument is complicated. But we could surely do a lot better with this one. Here is one way—not the only way—to do it:

> (3) The equal rights amendment should be defeated. There are two main reasons for this. First, (4) women should not have to fight in wars. Second, (1) it would be a mistake to abolish all laws that differentiate between men and women, since (2) women need special protection against various forms of exploitation, and since (5) in divorce cases the child should go with the mother, unless the court finds her incompetent or undesirable.

When a composition presents an extended argument, one of its conclusions may be the final one, in the sense that although it is supported by reasons, it is not itself used as a reason for any further conclusion. That assertion can be called the *thesis* of the composition. If there are several final conclusions, one may be more important than the others, or more heavily emphasized, or more central to the prevailing subject of the composition. That assertion can be called the *main thesis* of the composition.

EXERCISE 1B

Underline all the conclusions in the following arguments. Diagram the arguments and rewrite those that you can make more orderly.

1. The speed limit should be kept down to fifty miles per hour on all highways, because the supplies of oil should be conserved and every mile per hour of speed equals one thousand more deaths a year.

2. Busing children to schools out of their own neighborhoods is tiring to them, which is why busing is objectionable, and, consequently, why busing should be prohibited by federal law. It's also true,

and relevant, that busing excerbates the friction between racial and religious groups.

3. Moving television cameras onto the floor of Congress would be a disservice to democratic processes. It would lengthen debates, thus making Congress even less efficient, since it would encourage the windiest senators to sound off in prime time. And the general public would be discouraged to know how poorly Congress conducts itself.

4. The Cuban government poses no threat to American security, so there is no reason to continue the boycott on Cuban goods. It is clear that the Cuban government has no intention or capacity to injure the United States. It is also clear that the continuance of the boycott is producing increasing friction with our other Latin American neighbors.

5. Strip mining must be carefully regulated by Congress, for it produces enormous wastes of farm and forest land, it consumes enormous quantities of precious water, and it uproots many people from homes they have lived in for a long time—which, incidentally, also shows that the pending bill guaranteeing adequate compensation for homes should be passed promptly.

EXERCISE 1C

Suppose that you have the following beliefs about the proposed equal rights amendment (ERA) to the Constitution, which guarantees equal treatment under the law to men and women. Diagram their logical relationships, and consider how they are best deployed in an argument. Write an essay setting forth the argument.

1. Women should not be made liable, like men, for military service.

2. Paying women on the same basis as men would produce neuroses in men who feel it is their duty to bring home the bacon.

3. Women should not be deprived of their present legal privileges, such as not having to serve on juries and not having to pay alimony.

4. The stability of the social order depends on preserving traditional ways of acting.

5. Giving women more legal rights will discourage marriage.

6. ERA should not be ratified.

7. Promoting the equality of the sexes would weaken the institution of the family.

8. Making men and women equally liable for military service would destroy true femininity.

9. Women should not be given the same pay as men who do the same work.

10. Established social customs should not be weakened by new laws.

EXERCISE 1D

The following composition is in need of rewriting, partly because it violates the Rules of Grouping and Direction. Improve it.

Artists today are obviously only interested in one thing: making money by fooling the public—otherwise, why would they give us such wild, crude, meaningless paintings? That's why I say that art is a put-on, as phony as a three-dollar bill or packaged cereals. Look at the prices that the rich are paying for large canvasses with nothing on them but a few thin lines or dripping blotches of color—a far cry from Rembrandt and Raphael. Art has become a slave to fashion; new styles have to be invented every few years, like dress-designs or car-models. The present state of art is obviously degenerate. We must start reeducating the artistic taste of our children so they know what art really is, because that's the only way to get back to our old established values. Why, I saw a so-called painting the other day that was entirely black; and they called that a work of art!

TRUE OR FALSE?

propositions

It is true that

The Declaration of Independence was signed in 1776.

It is false that

The Declaration of Independence was signed in Boston.

What kind of thing is it that *can* be true or false? A *proposition*. I have just presented two different propositions, one of which is true, the other false. We cannot, on the other hand, say that

signed in Boston

is true, or that

1776

is false. Some series of words can be true or false; others cannot. Any series that can be true or false shall, for the purposes of this book, be called a *proposition*; and only a series of this sort shall be called a proposition.

You don't have to know *whether* a series of words is true or is false before you can tell that it is a proposition; you only have to know that it is the sort of thing that can sensibly be called "true" and "false." Most simple declarative sentences are propositions.

Napoleon Bonaparte won the Battle of Waterloo

is false; therefore it is a proposition. Any simple declarative sentence is a proposition if it satisfies two conditions: (1) it refers to something definite (its *referent*), and (2) it ascribes a determinate property to that referent. The sentence about Napoleon satisfies both conditions. First, the subject "Napoleon" refers to a particular historical figure, whom we can identify well enough—say, with the help of an encyclopedia—so that we can be confident that we are referring to the same person when we use this name. (Other persons have no doubt been named "Napoleon Bonaparte" —dogs, too. But if we just use the name without further ado, we are referring to the famous one, the Corsican, 1769–1821, who became a French general and Emperor of France.) Second, what the sentence says *about* Napoleon is that he won the Battle of Waterloo, and this phrase "won the Battle of Waterloo" is clear enough, since Wellington's victory was quite decisive and Napoleon's army surrendered. (Some battles don't end all that decisively, in which case it might not be true that one side either won or lost.)

Some simple declarative sentences, then, may fail to be propositions, either because the reference is not definite or because the predicate term is not determinate (it may be extremely vague, so we don't understand what we would be committed to if we were to say that the sentence is true or that it is false). Very many sentences, of course, rely on their context to make them definite and determinate. If the subject of the sentence is a pronoun, then either some previous sentence must explain what or whom it refers to, or else the circumstances under which it is spoken must supply the information (someone is being pointed at in court: "He is the man I saw!"). And many predicates would be intolerably indeterminate apart from a verbal context or life situation in which a good deal is taken for granted by those present (a remark that the weather is "hot" is understood to mean something like "hot for this time of year").

It is of the utmost importance for a writer to make sure his sentences really are propositions. When you write a composition, you are always writing *for* someone—that is, you must have at least some idea of a likely or possible reader, and you must make some assumptions about how much he knows about the subject you are discussing. If you refer to "The Who," the reference may be clear to some readers, but other readers may need help. Consider this excerpt from testimony that Casey Stengel once gave to a Congressional committee:

> I don't think anybody can support minor league baseball. . . . Softball is interesting. The parent is interested: he goes around with him. He watches his son and he is more enthusiastic about the boy than some stranger that comes to town and wants to play in a little wooden park and with no facilities to make you be interested. You might rather stay home and see a program. . . .
> Later on Mr. Rickey came in and started what was known as what you would say numerous clubs, you know in which I will try to pick up this college man, I will pick up that college boy, or I will pick up some corner lot boy, and if you picked up the corner lot boy maybe he became just as successful as the college man, which is true.
> He then had a number of players. . . .

Casey Stengel may have been able to make all this clearer by gesture and tone of voice, but imagine a composition in this style: it would be very difficult for the reader to disentangle the propositions that the writer may have had in mind.

Some propositions appear as grammatical units; others are buried in larger sentential constructions.

> Napoleon, the great French general, was short in stature and temper.

Here, the phrase in apposition to "Napoleon" constitutes a second proposition besides the main one. What is said is that:

1. Napoleon was short in stature and temper.
2. Napoleon was a great French general.

I'm not suggesting that you should write only simple declarative sentences—this is only a way of exhibiting plainly the two propositions whose truth or falsity may have to be considered. Or are there more than two propositions here? Instead of the first one, we could separate the two adjectives and write:

1'. Napoleon was short in stature.
1''. Napoleon had a short temper.

In this way, we make two propositions out of proposition 1. We can do so, but we don't have to. Proposition 1 is logically equivalent to 1′ plus 1″ in a sense to be explained in due course. We can analyze the original sentence either way—as containing two propositions or three. Which way we do it will depend on the larger verbal context—what sort of inference the sentence is to enter into. More on that later.

From the logical point of view, a piece of writing can be considered as consisting of a string of propositions. That's not all it is, by any means; nor is the logical point of view the only important one to adopt. But if we are interested in drawing reasonable inferences, and in making arguments that will convince others by getting them to draw reasonable inferences, we have to be concerned with propositions. Propositions are what we believe, when we believe something. The conclusion of an argument is a proposition; and a reason offered in support of that conclusion is also a proposition. So when we consider a piece of writing from the logical point of view, we want to know exactly what propositions it contains. And when we are writing informatively for others—describing, explaining, arguing—we want to make sure that what we write contains exactly the propositions we have in mind.

This way of regarding discourse brings out the importance of the comma in distinguishing between restrictive and nonrestrictive clauses. What is the difference between these two sentences?

> The police arrested the demonstrators who had sat down in the street.
> The police arrested the demonstrators, who had sat down in the street.

The second sentence consists of two propositions: (1) that the demonstrators referred to (presumably the verbal context would have made the reference definite) had sat down in the street, and (2) that the police arrested them. The first sentence, however, is but a single proposition, for the words "who had sat down in the street" here serve to help identify which demonstrators were arrested. The first sentence thus suggests that some of the demonstrators sat down and some did not; the second sentence suggests strongly that *all* the demonstrators who were present sat down. That comma makes a considerable difference to the sense.

A proposition can be embedded in a sentence by way of a definite description that refers to it, even though obliquely. Consider:

> My argument against Mother's Day is that it is commercialized.

This sentence is an argument; but what argument is it? The reason is stated in so many words: "Mother's Day . . . is commercialized." The conclusion has to be guessed at from the word "against": but probably, in context, it is something like "Mother's Day should be abolished." Putting an argument in this condensed form is often convenient and reasonably clear. But there is a danger, as this example shows, that the exact nature of the conclusion may be clouded. When someone says he is "against" something, others have a right to ask him whether that means he thinks it should be abolished, or made illegal, or discouraged, or deplored, or what.

EXERCISE 2A

How many propositions are there in each of the following sentences?

1. No one with the slightest claim to a reputation for honesty could conceivably have sold worthless stock.

2. The importance of following due process is shown by the fact that many persons are convicted of crimes they did not commit.

3. How deep is the ocean? How high is the sky?

4. Stanley, whose earlier efforts to make gold out of cheese were unsuccessful, has now invented a perpetual motion machine.

5. Although there is no doubt that the railroad is bankrupt, its directors, incompetent as they are, are not legally liable.

6. Let us be thankful for small blessings!

7. Having been radicalized while at college, Jonathan is now becoming a conservative again.

8. The first president of the United States, Benjamin Harrison, was an able executive.

9. Damn the torpedoes! Full speed ahead!

10. Oh, what a fool am I!

All propositions are either true or false (whether or not we know which). But propositions differ from each other in all sorts of other ways. Some of these other differences are of no interest to the logician (who does not care, at least professionally, whether they are expressed politely or what they are about). Others are of great interest, because they make a difference in the way a proposition can enter successfully into an argument, either as a reason or as a conclusion.

Various distinctions will emerge as we move along, and their importance will be plain. At this point, it is appropriate to introduce two distinctions that are very basic. The first is that between those propositions that have other propositions as parts and those that do not have other propositions as parts. The difference is like that between a machine that has other machines as parts (for instance, a car contains various electric motors) and a machine (such as an electric motor) that may have many parts, but none of whose parts are themselves machines.

We can borrow a pair of grammatical terms to mark this distinction, using them, of course, in somewhat extended senses. A proposition that is composed of two or more propositions is a *compound proposition:*

You may stay to the end if you wish, but I'm leaving.

This contains the propositions "You may stay to the end if you wish" and "I'm leaving" (we can picture a situation in which the referents of the pronouns are made clear). They are compounded with the help of the word "but," which acts as a *logical connective* to bind the two propositions into one. A proposition that is not constructed from other propositions is a *simple proposition:*

I am leaving.

This proposition has parts, but its parts are not themselves propositions.

There are four basic logical connectives:

Logical connectives

(both) . . . and . . .
(either) . . . or . . .
if . . . (then . . .)
. . . if and only if . . .

The dots represent the propositions that would be connected and compounded. Some words are in parentheses to indicate that they are often omitted and left to be understood. Note that "but" does not appear on this list. The reason is simple: "but" is really a form of "and," though it also carries the suggestion that what follows it is somehow unexpected in the light of what has just been said. In our example, the speaker might have said:

You may stay to the end if you wish and I am leaving.

This was indeed part of what he did say—what "but" added was an emphasis on the contrast between the two actions of staying and leaving.

In our example, one of the propositions connected by "but" is itself a compound proposition, which might be written out a little more formally in this way:

If you wish (to stay to the end), (then) you may stay to the end.

The connective "if . . . then. . ." makes one of the two simple propositions, "You may stay to the end," dependent on the other, "You wish to stay to the end." Of course the speaker was not asserting either of these simple propositions; he was only asserting that *if* one is true, *then* the other is true. He might have chosen other, approximately synonymous expressions to make his assertion, for example:

You may stay to the end unless you don't wish to stay to the end.

This does not mean exactly what was meant by the original compound proposition, but it is very close, logically speaking. "If . . . then . . ." propositions (and those that are synonymous with them) are called *conditional propositions*, or sometimes *hypothetical propositions*.

The connective ". . . if and only if . . ." is not as familiar as the others; it is not common in everyday talk. But it is valuable in composition, when it becomes necessary to make a certain logical relationship clear. Suppose you want to say that a conditional proposition is true in both directions. This is rarely the case, of course. When someone says:

To resign now would be to admit my guilt,

he certainly is saying:

If I resign now, then I am admitting my guilt.

But he is *not* saying:

If I admit my guilt, then I am resigning now.

So these two conditional propositions are not true in both directions. But suppose you want to say both of the following things:

> If Jones pays the ransom, the kidnapper will release him.
> If the kidnapper releases him, Jones will pay the ransom.

These can be combined as follows:

> The kidnapper will release Jones if and only if he pays the ransom,

or

> Jones will pay the ransom if and only if the kidnapper releases him.

Propositions compounded by "... if and only if ..." are called *bi-conditional*. And they can be used to combine pairs of the following sort as well:

> If Jones vouches for Smith, then I will hire him.
> If Jones does not vouch for Smith, then I will not hire him.

Both of these propositions are conveyed if you write:

> I will hire Smith if and only if Jones vouches for him.

The second basic distinction to be considered in this section is that between *affirmative* and *negative* propositions. In the simplest cases, the distinction is clearly marked by the absence or presence of the word "not" in the verb. The proposition

> The sky is blue

is affirmative: it ascribes a certain color to the sky.

> The sky is not green

is negative: it denies a certain color of the sky. Of course, trickier cases occur. One complication is that words and phrases can be negative, as well as propositions. There is "excusable" and there is its negative, "inexcusable." There is "regular" and there is "irregular." There is "happy" and there is "unhappy." But grammar is not always a reliable clue: "ravel" and "unravel" mean the same. We can write:

> Carlyle was not happy.
> Carlyle was unhappy.

Still, our basic distinction is to be preserved. The first proposition is negative, because "not" goes with the verb; the second is affirmative, though it has a negative term in the predicate.

"Not" may turn up at various places in a proposition: to decide whether the proposition is negative or affirmative, you have to think what "not" really goes with. In

> Not all lovers are blind,

the "not" goes with the verb. What the sentence says could be paraphrased this way:

> Some lovers are not blind.

But in

> Dogs are animals that are not very independent,

the "not" belongs with the predicate, not the verb, and the proposition is affirmative.

It is sometimes less easy to decide whether a compound proposition is affirmative or negative. In Chapter 10, this matter is made a good deal clearer. As we shall see, any compound proposition can be denied, and if it is affirmative, then its denial is a negative proposition. But this will need further explanation. In the meantime, it will be sufficient to note the distinction and keep it in mind. For it is fundamental—as is shown by one further consideration. When you assert that the sky is blue, you are at the same time affirming the truth of the proposition "The sky is blue." When you assert that the sky is *not* blue, you are affirming the *falsity* of the proposition "The sky is blue." In all kinds of composition, and at all times in writing, you must be very clear in your own mind whether you are saying that a proposition is true or saying that a proposition is false. There must be no confusion about that. What is equally important, you must make it clear to the reader which sort of thing you are saying. And this is done by judicious management of that little word "not." Place the "not" where its function is evident; don't, for example, write

> All those who saw the play did not enjoy it.

If you want to say that there were people who saw the play but did not enjoy it, you can write:

Not all of those who saw the play enjoyed it (negative).

If you want to say that there was no one who saw the play and enjoyed it, you can write:

All those who saw the play failed to enjoy it (affirmative).

The negative-affirmative distinction is also crucial in forming a topic sentence—that is, a sentence that sums up succinctly the central idea of a paragraph. Especially if you begin the paragraph with a topic sentence, and continue with reasons for it or illustrations of it, the reader will want to know whether you are for or against a particular proposition. And if you end the paragraph with a topic sentence, the reader will be expecting your summary to leave him in no doubt that you are in favor of capital punishment, rather than opposed to it, or that you are in favor of *abolishing* capital punishment, rather than opposed to its abolishment.

EXERCISE 2B

Label each of the following propositions as (1) simple (S) or compound (C) and (2) affirmative (A) or negative (N).

1. Not every driver with a parking sticker will find a place in the parking lot, even if he tries hard.

2. The company may decide to expand; on the other hand, it may not.

3. Judo is less violent and aggressive than Karate.

4. The non-dues-paying members present are asked to be nonvoters.

5. We can finance the campaign, provided our supporters contribute generously.

6. They toil not; neither do they spin.

7. To err is human; however, to forgive is divine.

8. There is nobody who can play the mouth organ like Ziggy.

9. Robert will take the job if it pays well.

10. Robert will not take the job even if it pays well.

EXERCISE 2C

Select a newspaper editorial on a topic that interests you—preferably one whose thesis you disagree with. Extract from it, and list in order, the propositions it contains, noting which are given as reasons for other propositions. Comment on the difficulties you encounter in trying to decide exactly what propositions are actually being asserted, whether they are simple or compound, and whether they are affirmative or negative. In the light of this analysis, rewrite the editorial in your own way, so that the propositions and their logical relationships are as clear as you can make them.

EXERCISE 2D

The following paragraph assembles a number of propositions that are apparently connected, but it has no topic sentence. Construct a topic sentence that best seems to sum up the point of the passage, and rewrite the passage in two ways, first with the topic sentence at the beginning, second with the topic sentence at the end. Notice how this shift calls for changes in the order of the other sentences.

City planners have come up with many grandiose schemes for rebuilding and reorganizing our cities. Much public money has been spent in designing pedestrian malls, central squares, high-rise apartment complexes, etc., many of which have never been built. Houses that were old, yet capable of being saved and lived in, have been torn down to make way for parking lots. Elegant old firehouses, railway stations, banks, etc., have given way to superhighways. Happy neighborhoods, ethnically united, where people have lived for many decades, have been broken up. Planning commissions have arbitrarily limited architects in their work by forbidding certain designs. Bribery and corruption have made sure that friends of the municipal government are allowed to do what they wish. Cold, barren, empty spaces, with a few droopy potted plants, have replaced corners and squares with outdoor markets and the bustle of human life.

THE ART OF PIGEONHOLING

classification

What do the jet set, the animals in a zoo, the Seven Wonders of the World, the twelve labors of Hercules, the United Nations, and the dramatis personae of *A Midsummer Night's Dream* have in common? Not much, if you are looking for concrete properties. But something quite basic, if you are interested in abstractions: they are all *classes*. This word has a number of senses in English, most of which we shall set aside here: for example, the jet set no doubt have a touch of class that is lacking in more humble persons; and those who meet periodically in a classroom to study Egyptology or ceramics are a class in another narrow sense. Here, however, a class is just all the individual things—which may be persons, objects, or events—that share a determinate property. This is the logical sense of the word.

Many things in the world are green, or dangerous, or tasty, or morally admirable: each of these properties distinguishes its own appropriate class. There is the class { green things } —the braces are for clarity in marking out classes. Each particular green thing in the world is a member of this class—which is sharply separated from the class { things that are in no way green } , such as the White House, pieces of Swiss cheese, the Battle of Waterloo, and the Constitution of the United States. (Metaphorical senses of "green"—such as "the greening of America" —are set aside in the present context.)

A great deal of our most valuable thinking involves classes and their logical relationships. There is perhaps nothing more important to be clear about, and to master, if you want to think well. Now when you take a close look in this chapter at classes and their connections, you will find much that is familiar, in a way. You are constantly thinking in terms of classes. But you will also find, I believe, that you will have a some-what better grasp of the essential distinctions than you had before; later, your thinking will become sharper, quicker, and more reliable because you are noticing and paying more attention to the logic of classes.

The basic relationships between classes are three: overlapping, ex-clusion, and inclusion. There is a fourth one, identity, but, as we shall see, it is derived from the others. (The relationship between { dogs } and Lassie, remember, is not between two classes, but between a class and one of its members.)

One class *overlaps* another when they have at least one member in common. If Jones and Smith belong both to the Kiwanis Club and to the Masonic Order, then the class { members of the Kiwanis Club } and the class { members of the Masonic Order } overlap. Circles tell the story:

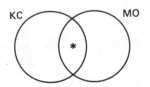

The asterisk calls attention to the fact that the area where the two classes intersect is occupied by at least one member, perhaps more (that question is left open). Class overlaps are a familiar and noteworthy part of our everyday experience: you, for example, have a great many distinct prop-erties—you may be tall, poor, a pianist, a student, and an apartment dweller. Each of these properties determines a specific class, and if all of those classes have (at least) you in common, then each of them over-laps each of the others.

One class *excludes* another if they do not overlap—that is, if they

have no members in common. No members of the Knights of Columbus
are also members of Hadassah, so these two classes exclude each other.
I am quite certain that no cats are dogs, and that no fish are birds (even
though there are "flying fish"). Exclusiveness is always mutual, of course,
since if one class excludes another, the other excludes it as well. Mutually
exclusive classes can be pictured this way:

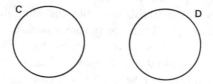

This diagram says, "Nothing is both a cat and a dog"—that is what my
labels mean. Class exclusiveness is a very important property in sorting
things out, as we shall see shortly. If the class { letters from Horace
Adams } and the class { letters from Janice Carr } were not mutually
exclusive, you would have a hard time devising a filing system for your
correspondence and deciding in which folder to place each particular
letter.

One class is *included in* another if every member of the first class
is also a member of the second class. Everyone who belongs to the
Daughters of the American Revolution (the DAR) is a woman, so the
class { DAR members } is included in the class { women } . The class
{ DAR members } is also included in the class { United States citizens
at least one of whose ancestors fought in the American Revolution } .
Here are the diagrams:

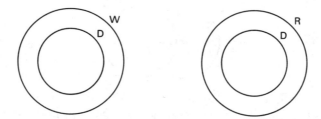

Class inclusion is easy to illustrate where clear biological relationships
have been established (cats are mammals), or where rules are laid down
(according to the Constitution, United States presidents have to be at
least thirty-five years old). Of course, we often do not know whether one
class is in fact included in another—say { local judges } and { honest
judges } .

Two classes are *identical to* each other when each is included in the other—in which case, they are not really two classes, but one. This is comparatively rare, no doubt, but it happens, and when it happens it is worth noting. Suppose that all the gray books in your library are books on existentialism, and all the books on existentialism are gray. Then the classes { gray books in your library } and { books in your library on existentialism } are the very same classes, under two different descriptions—that is, they have exactly the same members. That is a coincidence. More often, class identity is the consequence of a rule (the Supreme Court justices are those persons appointed to the Supreme Court by a president) or a natural law (a physical object reflects images if and only if its surface is extremely smooth). It is logically valuable to know that class A is identical with class B, for that enables you to infer that certain things that are true of either must be true of the other; for example, if some members of A are blue, then some members of B must be blue too, since the As and the Bs are in fact the same things.

When one class A is included in a second class B, but does not exhaust it (since they are not identical), a distinction is immediately suggested. Take opals and gems. The class { opals } is included in the class { gems } . But some gems are not opals; so we have implicitly made a distinction between those gems that are opals and those gems that are not opals. We have divided the class { gems } into two subclasses: { opals } and { nonopals } . Nested circles can represent this result:

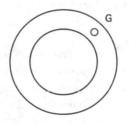

Within the smaller circle (O) we place the opals. Outside that circle, but still within the larger circle (G), we have left the gems that are not opals —diamonds, rubies, sapphires, emeralds, and the rest. This kind of division—which cuts a class neatly into two subclasses that are mutually exclusive but also completely exhaustive of the original class—is called a dichotomy.

The dichotomy is not the only kind of class division, as we shall see, but it is an extremely important kind, and worth attention. Notice what we have done, and what we have not done, in dividing $\{$ gems $\}$ into $\{$ opals $\}$ and $\{$ nonopals $\}$. We have not divided the class *equally*, for there are undoubtedly many more gems that are *not* opals than gems that *are* opals. We have not divided it in a way that would interest everyone, or that would be suitable for every occasion; if you were writing a composition on sapphires, for example, you would not be interested in our division at all. But we *have* divided it *completely*, in the sense that every gem you might run across will belong either in the class $\{$ opals $\}$ or in the class $\{$ nonopals $\}$. And we have divided it *cleanly*, in the sense that *no* gem can be put in both subclasses.

In a dichotomy, the two subclasses that exhaust the original class are *complementary classes:* everything in the class of gems that does not belong to one of the subclasses must belong to the other. We might have started with a broader class than the class of gems; indeed, we might have started with the broadest class of all, $\{$ everything $\}$. This includes whatever you can think of, and any class we might name dichotomizes it. There are opals and there is everything else—all things that are not opals, whether or not they are gems. For some logical purposes, we need to make use of this biggest class of all, $\{$ everything $\}$. But for most logical purposes, smaller classes will serve well enough. Philosophers talk about everything, and that is part of their job; most of us are not concerned with everything, but with such classes as people, items of food, bills, laws, rights, careers, and so on. These classes are quite broad enough to give us plenty to think about. They can clearly be divided in innumerable ways, and so we will often have to decide which is the best way to divide them (for some purpose we have in mind), and how best to do it.

As I have remarked, much of the time you are talking about classes of things, whether you realize it or not—the first sentence of the Declaration of Independence, for example, refers to such classes as $\{$ human events $\}$, $\{$ peoples $\}$, $\{$ political bands $\}$, $\{$ Laws of Nature $\}$, and $\{$ opinions of mankind $\}$. Not that the Declaration of Independence marks off these classes with braces; the braces are only an artificial device which I use here to emphasize certain basic logical relations. I do not suggest that you include them in your compositions. Instead of $\{$ human events $\}$, you can write "the class of human events," or just "human events." Nevertheless, you will sometimes find it clarifying, in working out your ideas, to use braces to mark out classes (especially complicated ones like the class of all childless married couples of whom one or both have attended at least two years of college), in order to keep them distinct.

EXERCISE 3A

Label the following pairs of classes according as they overlap (O), they exclude each other (E), or one is included in the other (I).

1. foxes / vixens
2. radishes / carrots
3. bachelors / unmarried adult males
4. SAR (Sons of the American Revolution) / males
5. SAR / females
6. hauberks / armor
7. poets / philosophers
8. Plymouths / sedans
9. crimes / homicides
10. villanelles / poems

We are surrounded by a bewildering variety of things, and we would be utterly unable to cope with them if we could not sort them out. To sort is just to assign to various classes—as when you get the dirty clothes ready to wash. Fortunately, our language is a sorting system of a kind; everytime we learn a new *general term* ("yawl," "lucid," "to mediate"), we acquire the concept of a new class that we can use in sorting out some of the things that come our way. And when we discover new and important differences between things, we can make up new words to label the classes involved (such as "stagflation"—a special class of economic conditions).

Now, suppose your interest is centered in a particular class of things, and you are trying to understand something about the things in that class. You are studying United States foreign policy actions during the cold war period, the pros and cons of offshore oil-well drilling, or the ethical problems raised by medical experimentation on persons confined in state penitentiaries. You may read up on the subject, or make your own firsthand investigation. As you learn more and more, you must begin to sort out what you know—because organizing the data will help you remember them, but also because the very process of sorting will reveal interesting new connections among the data.

In sorting, you choose which class to put each item into. Here is a soiled sock: it is (among other things) both small and dark. Should you put it with the handkerchiefs, because it is small, or with the sport shirts because it is dark? Actually, it belongs to both classes, and so it *can* be assigned to either. In this case you have a practical reason for making a choice: you put it with the dark clothes because its color may run in the washing machine if the water is too hot. Sometimes you may have a theoretical reason for a sorting. Sometimes you may have no reason at all—in which case the choice is arbitrary.

Before you can sort, you must have a set of classes in mind to work with—the classes to assign things to. You need a classification system. Classifying consists in selecting the classes to use in sorting some given class. A classification is a set of classes selected for the purpose of sorting.

The dichotomy is the simplest form of classification:

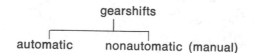

This diagram, with branching lines, is a handy one for setting forth a classification. But note what it says and what it doesn't say. It says that the class {gearshifts} can be divided into the two subclasses {automatic gearshifts} and {manual gearshifts}. It does not tell us whether there are any such things; we might, for example, have proposed another classification:

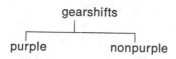

What's the difference between the two classifications? Two, actually: (1) in the second classification, one of the subclasses is empty (there are no purple gearshifts), which detracts a bit from the usefulness of such a classification—though it doesn't make it completely useless, by any means, since many valuable classifications may turn out to have some subclasses with no members; (2) it is easy to think of good reasons for distinguishing between automatic and manual gearshifts (for example, you might be able to use one but not the other); but it is not easy to think of a good reason for distinguishing between purple gearshifts and the rest. So the first classification might turn out to be significant, but the second one might not.

Since a classification does not commit itself to saying that the subclasses are actually occupied, it is an abstract scheme. And to emphasize this point, the various classes, subclasses, subsubclasses, and so on, are called *categories*. Categories are like the pigeonholes that might be set up in a small village post office for sorting incoming mail. Let's say we have one pigeonhole for each street. Now it may be that on a given day, or even for a week, nobody on Panama Street receives any mail—so that pigeonhole remains empty. But it is there in case we need it. And the categories of a classification scheme are ready and waiting in the same way; they provide a place to put things that may turn up in our experience, though we can't predict for certain what will in fact turn up.

The categories of a classification are arranged in various *ranks*, or levels. The two classifications we have exhibited so far are very modest: they have only two ranks. Here is a more ambitious one:

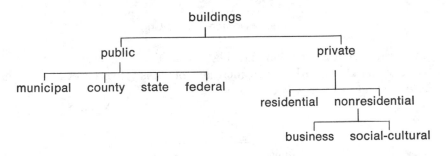

This is sketchy, but it will serve our purposes. Here are eleven categories, arranged in five ranks. The categories in each rank are said to be *subordinate to* those just above them (they are subclasses). And the categories in each rank are said to be *coordinate with* those on the same rank. So the categories of municipal buildings (for example, a city hall), county buildings (a county courthouse), state buildings (a state office building), and federal buildings (a mint) are coordinate categories of public buildings.

The buildings in each rank are divided from each other by reference to a particular property, which is the *basis of division* at that rank. The basis of division that gives us the four coordinate categories just mentioned is *level of government ownership*. That which divides residential from nonresidential buildings can only be somewhat awkwardly formulated as *whether or not people live there*, since we don't have a special term for it. But the distinction is reasonably clear, I think: the residential category would include private homes, apartment houses, dormitories, hotels; the nonresidential category would include factories, department stores, libraries, churches. And the basis for dividing the nonresidential buildings into two broad categories would be something like *type of function for which used*; although there is an indefinitely large variety of possible functions, our classification only goes so far as to separate the buildings that house primarily economic functions (factories, stores, banks) from those that house social and cultural functions (temples, Elks lodges, art museums).

The whole point of a classification system is that it introduces order. If it introduces more *dis*order than it clears up, its point is lost. So there are some rules to follow in classifying, and it is these rules that distinguish better classifications from worse ones.

Rule 1: *Use only one basis of division at each rank.* You may get away with violating this rule in the simplest cases:

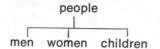

But even harmless violations are best avoided if you want to form the habit of thinking clearly. Since there are obviously two bases of division here, *age* and *sex*, it is better to write:

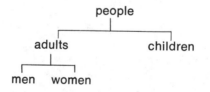

Or, the ranks could be reversed for some purposes:

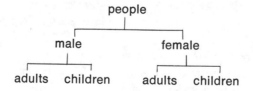

Which is better? That depends entirely on your guiding purpose—whether you need all seven categories or can get along with just five. If you are writing about an aspect of the legal system, and discussing the differences in the ways people are treated under the law, then the first classification may serve well, if you can ignore the distinction between male and female children. On the other hand, if you are writing about the United States census, its strengths and weaknesses, it may be safer to use the second classification, which provides pigeonholes for all the possible ways of dividing people, using only these two properties.

Rule 2: *Set up your categories so that they do not overlap.* When categories overlap, the same item can be assigned to both, and this is very confusing. Overlapping results from violations of Rule 1—though not all violations of Rule 1 lead to overlapping, as we have just seen in the men/women/children division.

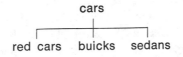

This would be hopelessly mixed up, worse than useless. There are three bases of division, all in the same rank—hence, categories that overlap considerably. Such a classification will not enable us to sort out cars.

Rule 3: *Make your bases of division as sharp as possible.* Simple bases of division, such as *color* and *make of car*, are quite sharp; there is no doubt about where to place each item that we want to classify—say, cars in a used-car lot. But sometimes the subject we are dealing with does not allow of sharp divisions; in such cases our bases of division are vague, even though they are the best we have. So there are borderline cases— items we are not sure how to classify. Take, for example, a building containing a storefront church and a coffee shop. Is it to be classified as "business" or as "social-cultural"? We may have to introduce special qualifications here, and speak of the *main* function of the building (versus its incidental uses, as when people made homeless by a flood are given shelter overnight in a church—which does not make the church a residential building). We may have to make a somewhat arbitrary ruling, just to keep our scheme in order: we stipulate that *any* building used for commercial purposes or manufacturing is to be classified as "business," no matter what else goes on in it. As long as we know what we are doing, and make clear to others what we are doing, no error or misunderstanding need result.

Rule 4: *Set up your categories so that they are as complete as desirable.* When I divided public buildings into four categories a while back, I tried to make my division *exhaustive*—that is, to provide a category into which every public building could find a place. I am afraid I overlooked foreign embassies in Washington and the United Nations headquarters in New York City. To make the classification of public buildings really complete, we should include categories for them, too. Now there is always a question of need here. If you are writing about governmental bodies within the United States, you need not include slots for foreign and international buildings in your classification. There is no use making the classification logically complete if it becomes unwieldy. On the other hand, there is often some advantage in stopping to think what categories you would need to add to make the scheme complete, because the effort may call your attention to some important items you hadn't thought of. What about my division into business and social-cultural buildings? Have I left anything out? What about private charitable institutions (say the Heart Association or Red Cross)? Well, I suppose these could go under the heading of "social-cultural"—that heading is, after all, pretty broad. It may also be rather loose, a kind of catch-all category for anything that isn't clearly a factory, store, office building, or banking institution. But of course if we are not satisfied with this category as it stands, we can subdivide it further, into another rank, and thus make clear just what we are and are not including in it.

socio-cultural nonresidential buildings

educa-tional (for example, the Franklin Institute Museum)	religious (St. Patrick's Cathedral)	social (Phila-delphia Athletic Club)	social service (a planned parenthood office)	social action (NAACP head-quarters)	political (Socialist Workers party head-quarters)

This set of categories is no doubt incomplete, add to it what you think necessary. And if you end up with inconveniently many categories in the same rank, you might try to think of ways of grouping them into larger categories.

It is well to keep in mind that an outline is also a classification: when you outline an essay before writing it, or outline an essay you have just read, you are classifying *ideas*. The principles of classification apply to outlines as to other classifications: you seek an organization that will provide a place, and only one right place, for each idea you have on hand; and you want the ideas that belong together to be grouped together under appropriate bases of division. Perhaps no more can be said in general about classifications. This general advice will not by itself tell you how to make a good classification in every case; but, if well heeded, it *will* help you avoid those most serious and crippling faults of classification that are at the same time faults of thinking.

EXERCISE 3B

Label those classifications below that use more than one basis of division (D), those that provide overlapping categories (O), and those that are incomplete (I)—that is, fail to be exhaustive.

1. apples / ripe, unripe
2. roses / red, white, pink
3. friends / those who borrow money from you, those who lend money to you, those who neither borrow nor lend
4. weather / pleasant, unpleasant
5. beliefs / true, unreasonable
6. educational institutions / colleges, universities, institutions including a medical school and law school, well-endowed institutions
7. promises / sincere, unkept
8. newspapers / Democrat, Republican, Independent
9. medicines to be taken orally / liquid, pills, capsules
10. government officials / appointed, elected

EXERCISE 3C

Devise a suitable classification scheme for the following things:

a shovel

a rosebush

a painting by Picasso

a butterscotch sundae

a French poodle

a pencil

a white house

a revolution

a pearl necklace

a bottle of wine

a state legislature

a Shakespeare sonnet

Write a short essay explaining your choice of bases of division and giving your reasons for putting two or more of the above items in the same category.

EXERCISE 3D

The following short composition is disorganized because some of the ideas are out of place. Outline the composition, noting the misplaced ideas, and rewrite it in a more orderly way.

A group of Pennsylvania power companies is proposing to set up a huge "Energy Park" in central Pennsylvania—that is, a concentration of five to ten nuclear power plants. These companies, some of which have already been fined for polluting the environment with fly ash and other particulate matter from their coal-burning plants, have purchased a great deal of land—they would need many thousands of acres for such a park. The whole thing is being kept secret so that environmentalists will not discover until too late what is being done—though a great deal of cooling water will be required for each Park, and will deprive a large area of needed water that is needed for fishing, drinking, and other purposes.

The sponsors claim that the Energy Park will create new jobs. It will also create much bitterness when the residents of the area hear about it. For it will affect nature profoundly in that area, mainly through the enormous quantities of waste heat that will be poured into the environment, the large quantities of sulfur dioxide, and the particulate matter. These can affect health, and change the weather. No wonder the Montour County Commissioners, where the plant is proposed, have voted against it.

There is also the danger of radioactivity, which is bound to be released in such a large project. And sulfur dioxide can seriously affect lung and heart conditions, as well as turn into sulfuric acid, which forms the "acid rains" that have retarded crops and forest growth in many areas, kill aquatic life, and corrode even stone buildings.

4

SAYING WHAT YOU MEAN

definition

Many arguments that are somewhat complex involve one or more definitions. Indeed, the point of the argument might be to convince someone that he ought to accept a certain definition. But even when definitions don't play quite so central a role, they may be indispensable. So if you want to argue well, you have to know how to present definitions —and also how to handle definitions proposed by others.

To begin with: what is a definition? Judging from the variety of things that have been called "definitions," the answer to this question is not as widely known as you might think. It will be well to frame that answer with some care.

The first thing to note is that what we define are *terms*—that is, words or phrases—not *things*. You can't, strictly speaking, define a horse or horses; but you can define the word "horse" or the phrase "stalking horse," as it is used idiomatically. Keeping this simple but basic distinction in mind will save you a good deal of confusion. For when you set out to define "democracy," say, or "socialism," or "socialist democracy," there are a great many interesting things you might want to say. But not all of these things belong in the definition. Remember that it is the *term* "socialist democracy" that you are concerned with, not the system of government itself: that will help you focus your attention (and your reader's attention) on the properties that need to be mentioned in the definition.

The distinction between talking about words and talking about other things can hardly be overstressed. Compare these two propositions:

> Five is a number.
> "Five" has one syllable.

The first proposition is about the number itself—it is a truth of arithmetic. The second proposition is not about the number five, but about the word "five"—it is a truth of linguistics. Note that I enclose a word in quotation marks to show that I am referring to the word itself rather than using the word to refer to something else:

> Carla is pretty.
> "Carla" is a girl's name.

Italics are often used for the same purpose, and that convention is also acceptable, as long as it is understood:

> *Five* has one syllable.
> *Carla* is a girl's name.

Both quotation marks and italics have other uses, so there are opportunities for confusion. That's why I sometimes write:

> The word "five" has one syllable.
> The name "Carla" is a girl's name.

What is true of a word is seldom true of what the word stands for, and vice versa. Many things may be true about socialist democracy; quite different things are true about the term "socialist democracy"— for example, it has seven syllables and is in iambic meter. But these features of the term are not what interest us in definition, of course; the definition purports to tell us the *meaning* of the term. When you frame a definition, make clear that you are talking about the term you are defining (the *definee*), not about the thing it refers to.

A definition, then, declares meaning, but it does so in its own way:

by presenting us with another term (the *definer*) that has the same meaning as the definee. Moreover, a definition does not merely give us a single word that is a synonym of the definee:

"Liberty" means the same as "freedom."

(This is not strictly a definition.) Rather, it gives us a breakdown of the meaning of the definee, distinguishing the meanings that are parts of that meaning:

"Benedict" means the same as "recently married man who had previously been a bachelor for some time."

To break down a complex meaning in this way is like presenting a partial classification:

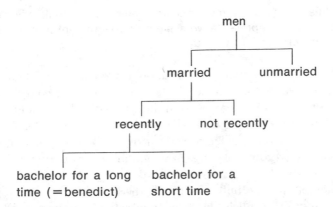

Since a definition gives us a definer that purports to have the same meaning (or at least one same meaning) as the definee, it is a rule of substitution. We can substitute the definee and the definer for each other in ordinary propositions:

Jones is a *benedict.*
Jones is a *recently married man who had previously been a bachelor for some time.*

The definition also sharpens our understanding of the concept of what it is to be a benedict, for it shows that in order to be properly called a "benedict," one must (1) be a man, (2) be recently married, and (3) have been a long-time bachelor.

This is in essence what a definition is. We must also note what it is not. First, it is not a proposition, even though it may be stated in a declarative sentence. It is a *rule of language:* it tells us how the term is to be used. In this respect it is like a rule of a game, such as tennis or bridge. The tennis player must not step on the base line in serving; the bridge player must follow suit. These are rules you have to obey in order to play the game. So a definition is an announcement, so to speak, that the writer intends to follow a certain rule (he intends to use a certain term in a certain way); better, it is a commitment to follow the rule.

Now if the rule that is announced in a definition is actually the one that is generally followed by users of the language, the definition is *correct*—like the definition of "benedict" (for this is the way the dictionary defines the term, and the dictionary is supposed to report prevailing usage). If a writer decides to attach a wholly new meaning to a term, then his definition is not correct; but it may be acceptable if it is clear and useful. He might lay down his rule this way:

> In this essay, the term "socialist democracy" shall have the same meaning as "representative system of government in which all goods are the property of the state."

And if he follows his own rule throughout, we can't deny him the privilege of using words the way he wants to use them. Of course, when you deviate from ordinary usage, or from the usage of scholars and specialists, you take the risk of being misunderstood. Ordinarily, a democracy does not have to be a representative system of government (it might be like the New England town meeting, in which all voters participate directly); and a socialist society need not socialize all property, but only the means of production and the bulk of capital. In this case the writer was well advised to be very explicit about his own rule of language; and it would be even smarter, probably, for him to note just how and where his usage differs from that of others.

A definition is not a metaphorical description, such as:

> "Philosophy" may be defined as "searching in the dark for a black cat that isn't there."

However apt this unkind remark may seem, it is not strictly a definition of the word "philosophy"; it is simply an attempt at a witty characterization of the philosopher's quest.

A definition is not an example, or a series of examples:

> "Philosopher" means someone like Plato, Aristotle, and John Dewey.

Giving examples to help people understand the meaning of a term is often a valuable recourse—and sometimes the only recourse. Even if you can't offer a definition of a term, because you haven't thought out exactly what it means, you may be able to establish communication with the help of some clear examples. By reflecting on the examples and on what they have in common, your reader can grasp some of the meaning of the term in question. From six well-chosen examples of, say, Georgian architecture, a perceptive observer might get quite a good idea of what is meant when a building is said to be in that style. Still, giving examples is not defining, and examples will not fully serve when a definition is wanted.

But when is a definition wanted? On various occasions, but principally when there is danger of misunderstanding. You may have a sound and forceful argument to offer. Yet if one of its key steps involves a term that your reader does not understand, he cannot follow your argument or be swayed by it until that gap is filled in. Now, you can't foresee the needs of all your readers, and you can't take the time to explain every word that might possibly give someone trouble. You can only try to follow two general, rough-and-ready, but valuable principles. First, when you find yourself using a term that is the technical term of some special field of interest or activity (whether molecular biology or surfing), some readers will not know what it means. And if it is important to you to reach those readers, you had better present a definition. Of course, if you are writing for the specialists—surfer to surfer, say—you can use the technical terms without qualm. If this book, for example, were addressed to logicians, it would require few definitions; but every technical term of logic in it is defined. Second, if you find it handy for your own purposes to introduce a new term of your own, or an old term in a new sense, then you must define it. For no one can be expected to grasp its meaning without help. Some of the terms I have chosen to use in this book—"definee" and "definer," for example—are made up just for convenience.

It isn't always necessary to state the definition formally:

> "Definee" means the same as "the term in a definition whose meaning is explained."

Sometimes the defining can be done casually, along the way, by putting words in apposition. Recall what was written above:

> So when you frame a definition, make clear that you are talking about the term you are defining (the *definee*), not about the thing it refers to.

That's one way of introducing a definition. But, of course, it also helps when the term chosen, though newly minted, has a certain appropriateness and is understood quite readily in the new sense by the reader.

EXERCISE 4A

Which of the following are definitions?

1. "Parent" means "one who has at least one child."

2. "To parent" means "to carry out the functions of a parent."

3. "Parenthood" means "the unremitting struggle to bridge the generation gap."

4. "Joke" means shaggy-dog stories, running gags, and the like.

5. "Bland" means "lacking in any definite flavor or character."

6. "Craven" means "fearful."

7. "Home" means "place where someone resides."

8. Anything that dates from a person's birth can be called "congenital."

9. "Philosophunculist"—in other words, "one who pretends to, or dabbles in, philosophy."

10. "Happiness is having a sturdy roof beneath your head." (Snoopy)

The three central questions about definition are these: What to define? When to define? How to define? I have suggested answers to the first two questions; now for the third.

The best that can be done briefly is to lay down some general principles or pieces of advice. Following them will not guarantee good definitions in every case, but will enable you to avoid the worst faults and help you frame definitions that will tend to serve, rather than frustrate, the purpose of defining—which is to make clear and explicit what it is that you mean to say. Here are six principles of definition:

1. Stick to a single sense. A definition declares a meaning. Most words have several meanings, or senses. Thus, strictly speaking, you define a word in one of its senses. We speak of a "*board* of directors" and of a "*board* nailed over a window"; these are two different senses of the word. There is no use looking for a definition of "board" that will cover both senses. Pick the sense you require for the argument you are making, and define the word in that sense. To make sure your reader knows which sense you are after, you can refer to the context in which that sense is usually operative: "board" as used in discussing corporations or universities; "board" as used by carpenters.

> "Board" (as used of corporations) means "official body."

Or instead of defining the single word, you can define the whole phrase containing it:

> "Board of directors" means "body with power to make ultimate decisions."

2. Get the grammar straight. Since a definition is, among other things, a rule permitting substitution, the definee and the definer must belong to the same part of speech. Never write:

> "Party" means "when a group of people get together for a good time."

Try substituting the definer for the definee in this proposition:

> A wild party next door kept me up all night.

The result would be nonsense. Adjectives are defined by adjectives, verbs by verbs, and so on.

3. Grasp the category. In our everyday thinking we sort out the endlessly varied things in our experience into very broad and basic categories.

Basic categories

objects
events
qualities
relations
abstract entities
living things
thoughts
propositions
persons

This list is far from complete, but it is long enough. Now when you define a term, you should always be clear, at least in your own mind, about what category it belongs to. Take "party" in the sense defined above. It refers to an event of a certain kind, something that happens—not an object or a quality. "Wild," on the other hand, refers to a quality, or property, of an event—or, in a different sense, to a property of a person. The number five is an abstract entity. Fatherhood is a relation between one person and another.

You don't always have to mention the basic category in your definition, though sometimes it is essential. If you define "Declaration of Independence," you should make clear whether you are referring to the piece of paper in Washington, D.C., to the set of principles embodied therein, or to a certain historical event. If the category is clear in your mind, chances are it will be clear to the reader; and you will probably be able to keep the grammar straight.

4. Narrow down the definer as far as you can. By "narrowing down," I mean adding qualifications so that the class of things referred to becomes smaller and smaller:

> house
> two-story house
> blue two-story house
> small blue two-story house
> small blue two-story split-level house
> small blue two-story split-level Colonial-style house.

Suppose you are defining "frisbee." Once you have the right category in mind (physical object), you ask what other properties frisbees have—properties that distinguish them from other physical objects. They are made of plastic, are saucer-shaped, are about ten inches across, and have a curving lip. Is that enough to enable someone to pick out a frisbee from a pile of miscellaneous objects? If so, you have the makings of an adequate definition. Sometimes you find that you can't narrow the class down as far as you'd like, so your definition is not complete; it is a partial definition, because it gives some, but not all, of those properties that belong to the meaning of the term you are defining. Still, even a partial definition may be useful—as long as it is understood to be partial.

5. Leave out unnecessary features. Would you define "bicycle" as "machine with six wheels and a smokestack"? Why not? Well, you might say, bicycles don't *have* smokestacks, so if you defined "bicycle" this way, you wouldn't pick out the right class of things. True, but suppose you put a smokestack on your bicycle; would it be any less a bicycle? The point is not that a bicycle doesn't (normally) have a smokestack but that it doesn't *have* to have a smokestack to be a bicycle. In defining, we are looking not just for any properties of the object, but for those properties that make it that kind of object rather than some other kind. Well, you might say, another thing wrong with the definition is that bicycles have two wheels, not six. Now we are on to something. The point is that a bicycle *has* to have two wheels to be a bicycle; that is a rule. Not a rule about bicycles (such as "Bicycles should have lights"), but a rule about how we are to use the word "bicycle."

When you define the word "chair," you can think of all sorts of properties that chairs have. But if only some chairs have them, not all, then these properties do not belong in the definition. (Otherwise, you will not have defined "chair," but rather "dining-room chair"—something too narrow). You should ask: Is this property something necessary to a chair? Would something lack it and still be correctly considered a chair? If the property is not necessary, leave it out.

6. Define less familiar words in terms of more familiar ones. This advice is fairly obvious. If you are defining a term because you fear that your reader does not understand its meaning (or at least the relevant meaning), you must find other words to define it—words that your reader is more likely to understand already. Sometimes this requires several stages, so you need a chain of definitions, by which you go from the technical terms of the original definee to less and less technical terms.

> "Catch" (in football) means "act of establishing player possession of a live ball in flight."
> "Live ball" means "ball in play."
> "In play" means "having been released by the center but not yet grounded."

A definition has to start with *some* words to use in its definer, and a chain of definitions can't go on forever. If you make sure the terms that appear in the definer are more accessible to your probable reader than the definee itself, you will also avoid one of the basic faults of definition— that is, trying to define a term in terms of itself. When this happens in a single definition, the definition is *circular*; and it is futile, for it doesn't explain the meaning of the definee unless you already know what it means—in which case you don't need the explanation at all. More often, circularity happens in a set of definitions. For example:

"Catch" (in football) means "act of establishing player possession of a live ball in flight."
"In flight" means "being in play but not yet caught."

Here, "catch" is defined in terms of "flight," and "flight" in terms of "catch" (or rather the past participle of "catch"). We have a circular definition-set.

EXERCISE 4B

What faults do you find in the following definitions?

1. "Envy" means "hostile feeling directed to someone else on account of his greater wealth."

2. "Fan" means "electrically powered device for stirring air."

3. "Tail" means "posterior appendage, or prolongation of posterior."

4. "Hassle" means "people getting all worked up over some disagreement."

5. "Broker" means "one who deals in the buying of stocks and bonds from, or in the selling of them to, private investors, other brokers, and investment houses."

6. "Boor" means "ill-mannered person."

7. "Tent" means "portable canvas shelter used in camping."

8. "Buckle" means "dessert that is a cross between a cake and a pudding."

9. "Cough drop" means "hard candy designed to alleviate coughing."

10. "Election" means "someone runs for office and people vote for or against him."

EXERCISE 4C

Select a subject that you have some special knowledge of (such as hockey, electronics, bluegrass music, astrology, or natural foods), and write an essay about it, defining as clearly and accurately as you can several important technical terms used by experts in that subject. Assume your reader knows nothing about it already.

EXERCISE 4D

The following passage from a composition is evidently an effort to clarify the meaning that the writer wishes his key word to have. Point out his violations of the proper procedures for defining, and rewrite the passage without those violations.

Certainly I agree with those who believe that a good education is essential to happiness. My reader will no doubt be surprised to hear this, because, in some sense or other, there are probably many people in the world with no education at all who are perfectly happy. But by "happiness" I mean leading a deeply satisfying and rich life, involving intellect and emotions, a life which obviously requires the development of the mind through study and learning. If my word "rich" be deemed too vague, I should explain that by a "rich life" I have in mind a life that does not consist only of passive enjoyment, like watching television, but involves areas of satisfaction that come from achieving one's goals, at least to the point at which one is happy with what one has achieved. So if you want to be a pianist, a painter, or a politician, you would have some success in that direction, and you couldn't do so without the right education.

MISUNDERSTOOD?

doubtful meaning

Communication between writer and reader can break down in two ways. The reader may simply fail to understand what the writer is saying; it is the chief function of definitions to remedy this situation. Or the reader may *misunderstand* what the writer is saying—that is, take him to be saying something different from what he is actually saying. What's worse, the writer can misunderstand himself: he thinks he is saying one thing but is actually saying something else. He may even think he is saying something definite when he is not, because his words have a doubtful meaning and can be understood in more than one way.

If you are interested in convincing someone by argument, you must know what you are really saying, and you must communicate. And if you wish to communicate, you must make sure that there can be no reasonable doubt about what you mean. We shall consider here three ways in which doubts about meaning can arise:

46

1. Doubtful reference.
2. Doubtful sense: ambiguity.
3. Doubtful degree: vagueness.

The problem of reference is just to give a sufficiently detailed description of whatever person, place, event, or object you wish to refer to so that your reader can pick it out with confidence. You wouldn't refer to "the musketeer," knowing that there were three musketeers; this description will not tell your reader which musketeer you are referring to. The name "New York" is OK if the context makes clear whether you are referring to the city or the state. "The Apostle James" could create confusion—since two of the Twelve Apostles were named James—unless you add "the son of Zebedee." But descriptions such as "the Muse of History," "the inventor of blood-plasma storage," "the author of *Hamlet*" are definite—they point to one and only one individual.

Mismanagement of pronouns can sometimes give rise to doubtful reference:

> Jones told Smith as soon as he could. He was glad to know the truth at last.

Was it Jones or Smith who was glad? It's a tossup. If your reader has to choose, and is smart, he will put his money on Smith. But you might have meant Jones, bursting as he was to impart the news he had so recently received. In any case, it would be safer to make the reference definite. You could write:

> As soon as he could, Jones told Smith, who was glad to know the truth at last.

Or:

> Jones, who was glad to know the truth at last, told Smith as soon as he could.

Doubtful sense, or ambiguity, is the source of endless confusion and misunderstanding. For example:

> Ivan is a Russian historian.

Does that mean that (1) Ivan is a historian who happens to be Russian, or (2) that Ivan is a specialist in Russian history? It could be either.

There are simply two meanings possible for "Russian historian." Apart from any context, then, the sentence is equally susceptible to two distinct interpretations, and there is no way of justifying one over the other; nor can the sentence mean both of these things at the same time. So neither of the two possible meanings is decisively set forth.

In such a case, we must not say that "Ivan is a Russian historian" is a proposition; it is a sentence that is in uneasy ambivalence, not quite either of two possible propositions. Nor should we say that the phrase "Russian historian" is a single term; a term is a word or phrase taken in a specific sense, and we do not know which of two possible terms "Russian historian" is until we can determine which sense it has.

A single word can be ambiguous in a certain context. If you write

There was some critical comment on the Colonel's speech,

your sentence is ambiguous, for "speech" could have two meanings. People might have been critical of the Colonel's way of speaking (his accent, perhaps), or of a particular address that he gave. These are not the same thing. Sometimes a whole clause or sentence is ambiguous, because of uncertainty about the grammatical relationships among its words.

John likes golf better than his wife

is almost perfectly balanced between two meanings; being elliptical, it can be filled in either way:

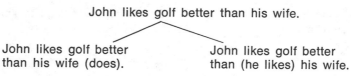

John likes golf better than his wife.

John likes golf better
than his wife (does).

John likes golf better
than (he likes) his wife.

The original ambiguous sentence splits into two unambiguous sentences, as we fill in the context a little more. This technique is called *disambiguating*—that is, rewriting the sentence in two (or more) ways, each of which fixes one of its possible meanings.

Nor is it only trivial remarks that can involve ambiguity. The Constitution of the United States provides that "No person except a natural born Citizen . . . shall be eligible to the office of the President." But what does "natural born" mean here? We can disambiguate this sentence easily enough:

No person except a natural born citizen shall be eligible to the Office of President.

| No person except one born a citizen (that is, born to parents who are citizens) shall be eligible to the office of President. | No person except one who is native-born (that is, born in the United States) shall be eligible to the office of President. |

The first step is to see the ambiguity; the next step is to resolve it, if that can be done. In this case the correct sense has not yet been ruled on by the federal courts; the ambiguity will no doubt remain until we have a presidential candidate who is "natural born" in one of the two senses but not in the other.

If the writers of the Constitution could fall into ambiguity, how much easier it is for the rest of us! Here are some sentences from student essays:

> Every salesman should know how to dress and approach a customer.
> I little realized why my ancestors came to America before I wrote this theme.
> Many people nowadays do not know much about the digestive system except that food is placed in the mouth and leaves by route of the rectum. This must be changed for a healthy and happy life.

In the first one, there is nothing to tell us whether "customer" or a tacitly understood "oneself" is the object of "dress." In the second, there is nothing to fix either the failure of realization or the immigration as what took place before the writing. In the third, that most unmanageable word "this" is up to its familiar mischief of failing to pin down its referent—which here was no doubt intended to be the general ignorance but (as far as the rest of the passage would indicate) might just as well be the present digestive process.

When you are really interested in what you want to say, you will find it worthwhile to take precautions against ambiguity. The best procedure is to set aside what you have written for a while, perhaps even a day or two, and then return to it, trying to read it as someone else might. If you can find someone to read it for you, all the better. When you come across an ambiguity, eliminate it. How do you do this? Most often by building up the context a little so that the word or phrase can be read in only one way:

Every salesman should know how to dress and how to approach a customer.

Before I wrote this theme, I little realized why my ancestors came to America.

... This ignorance must be changed for a happy and healthy life.

Even the rather shocking ambiguity of the sentence about John and his wife turned out to be quite easy to straighten out: by adding "does" at the end, we eliminated one of its possible senses; by adding "he likes" at the right place, we eliminated the other. Most ambiguities can be straightened out by judicious management of context. In other cases, we have recourse to an explicit definition:

When I use the word "speech" in this context, I mean the propositions set forth by the speaker.

If these resources fail, we can always substitute another term for the troublesome one. Instead of saying

Senator S—— is supporting Mayor M—— for Congress

(which might be taken to mean that the Senator is making financial contributions to the mayor's campaign), we might find it safer to write:

Senator S—— endorses (is in favor of) Mayor M——'s candidacy.

Vagueness is a kind of doubtful meaning, but is quite different from ambiguity. It pertains only to terms that have a decided sense but mean qualities that differ in degree rather than in kind. An animal is either a dog or not a dog; it is either all white or not all white. But it may be more or less fierce, more or less large, more or less intelligent. "Fierce," "large," and "intelligent" are words that refer to degree qualities; "dog" and "all white" are not. Vagueness arises because we can use these degree words in either of two ways, comparatively and absolutely:

My dog is fiercer than your dog. (comparative use)
My dog is fierce. (absolute use)

Since we know that fierceness is a matter of degree, we can always wonder about the absolute use of the term: how fierce is fierce? What one person (who is used to being around dogs) calls "fierce" is a fairly high degree of aggressiveness; mere loud barking and growling he considers mild behavior. What another person (who is rather timid about dogs) calls "fierce" is any canine behavior that seems slightly threatening. One man's "fierce" is another man's "forceful."

It's easy to see how misunderstandings occur with degree words. They are vague: that is, there is no general agreement as to how high a degree is required in order for a degree word to be applied absolutely. So, we may imagine a kind of scale along which dogs might be rated with respect to their aggressiveness:

very gentle ———————————— very fierce.

When Jones says a dog is fierce, he would place the dog at about the middle of this line, but when Smith says a dog is fierce, he would place the dog about three quarters of the way over.

If vague words were rare and easily avoided, they would present no great problem. But in fact most common degree words have some degree of vagueness, and some are vaguer than others. So there is always a problem, when you use one of these words ("rich," "intelligent," "courageous," "authoritarian," and so forth), of letting your reader know as precisely as you can what degree you have in mind. If a matter of degree can be transformed into a quantitative statement, that is often advisable: instead of saying someone is "rich," you can give his income, or approximate income, or say that he is in the top one percent of all millionaires. If no such measure is available, you can introduce a *standard of comparison:*

He is extremely intelligent, by which I mean that his intelligence is on the order of that of a Nobel prize-winning physicist.

How vague it is safe to be—or, conversely, how precise you should try to be—depends on the nature of the argument you are making. If the question is whether your neighbor should keep his dog confined, you don't have to fix the degree of fierceness very sharply to make out a good case. If it is a question whether a local obscenity ordinance should be declared unconstitutional, and the authorities ordered not to interfere with a showing of some controversial film, such as *Carnal Knowledge* or *Deep Throat*, then much more care may have to be taken. Many an ordinance has been thrown out by the courts because it contained undefined words such as "contrary to public morals" or "lewd and lascivious," which were left far too vague to be used in a law—since no one could be sure whether he was breaking the law or not.

EXERCISE 5A

Expose the ambiguity in each of the following sentences by rewriting the sentence in two unambiguous ways.

1. Nannie Doss gets life term for poisoning fifth husband.
2. Warns against abuse of fifth amendment.
3. Father of eleven fined $200 for failing to stop.
4. Doctor compiles list of poisons children may drink at home.
5. Boy critical after being hit by truck.
6. Save time and cut fingers with a parsley mincer.
7. Last week, his wife left him in a cheerful frame of mind.
8. For sale: one four-poster bed for antique lover.
9. The cigarette designed for men that women like.
10. Eat at Gary's restaurant, where the good food is an unexpected pleasure.

Confusions about the meanings of words can not only cause a breakdown in communication between writer and reader; they can also be fatal to the success of an argument. As an argument moves along from reasons to conclusions, perhaps in a long series of steps, its logical integrity depends on two things: it must keep to its subject and its line of thought, without wavering or wandering; it must not overreach itself by pulling out conclusions that go beyond the support that its reasons provide. When a key word or phrase secretly shifts its meaning in the course of an argument, the argument goes astray and fails to establish its conclusion.

The logical fault—a concealed shift of meaning in the course of an argument—is a serious one. It is not necessarily deliberate; often, the arguer is not aware that he is changing the meaning of an important word, and so he thinks he is proving something that he has not proved at all. He may fool his reader as well as himself—unless his reader is more alert than he is.

In principle, a shift in meaning can occur in any of three ways, corresponding to the kinds of doubtfulness we have just discussed. But the first kind would be unlikely. An argument *might* fail because it involves a shift of reference, so that what the conclusion talks about is not what the premises talk about. But such a violent logical lurch would be as hard to conceal as the inebriation of someone who can barely stand up. The third kind of shift—a shift in the degree of some quality—is somewhat more frequent, and worth brief comment.

Consider this example:

> Perkins, you have readily admitted, is certainly a competent painter; his showings have been well reviewed. But, then, why isn't his talent adequately recognized? As fine a painter as he should certainly have had his paintings purchased by the Whitney and the Metropolitan.

In a short space this kind of shift is hard to get away with, but in a longer passage it might not be noticed. The premise agreed upon is that Perkins is a *competent painter*. But this term is vague, and the precise degree of talent that it encompasses has not been fixed. So the arguer slides along the scale, and two sentences later he is describing Perkins as a *fine painter*. The conclusion (that his paintings should appear in major museum collections of contemporary American art) depends on the claim that Perkins is a fine painter, but this is not really warranted by the premise; he might be competent, but not fine.

Shifts of degree are particularly suited to the abuse of emotive language, as we shall see in the following chapter.

Shift of sense is the most common and troublesome kind: it is called *equivocation*. To see how it works, let us consider this absurdly simple case.

> Actors are men.
> Parsons is a poor actor.
> ∴. Parsons is a poor man.

No doubt, several faults could be found with this argument, but the point here is this: a word such as "poor" takes its specific meaning from the noun it is combined with, and in the course of this little argument it shifts from the context "poor actor" (meaning, no doubt, an incompetent actor) to "poor man" (meaning a man of little wealth).

The Parsons argument wouldn't fool anybody, but plenty of equivocations have. A more plausible one is this:

> As far as I am concerned, we need not pay any particular attention to the principal of the school when it comes to educational matters, because I don't see that he has any authority in education. He doesn't even have enough authority to keep the boys and girls behaving quietly in the lunchroom, which is frequently a place of bedlam.

This argument might be deceptive if it were spread out and toned up with more passionate language. Still, there is a very severe central shift in the meaning of "authority." When we speak of "authority" over the children in the lunchroom, we are speaking of power and the inclination to use it to keep them quiet. When we speak of someone as an "authority" in education, we mean that he has specialized knowledge in this field and that his views are therefore entitled to some respect. Because a person lacks authority in one sense, it by no means follows that he lacks authority in the other sense.

Once we notice the equivocation, and expose it by such an analysis as this, it loses its power to deceive. The argument, which at first may have had an air of convincingness, is now seen to be quite hollow, if not absurd.

EXERCISE 5B

Point out shifts of meaning in the following arguments, and explain in your own words the different senses or degrees involved.

1. Peanuts must be a basic necessity in our diet, and we should be sure to eat them regularly; for they are listed by the Department of Agriculture, along with rice, corn, cotton, wheat, and tobacco, as "basic crops."

2. I am in favor of our present college curriculum, which includes certain "basic studies" that are required of all students and that surely are very basic, such as English composition, language, and mathematical skills. Why then, are philosophy and religion not included? These surely deal with fundamental problems, and are basic systems of thought.

3. Well, the mayor has finally admitted publicly that there was some "irregularity" in the operations of his budget department last year —a charge that had been made and substantiated by the press. The gravity of the offense has not yet been acknowledged, however, and will not be suitably acknowledged until the mayor makes up his mind to resign. Certainly, any substantial irregularity in the city administration's financial dealings is sufficient to make the mayor unworthy of office.

4. I realize that some social critics are troubled by the extreme disparity of wealth in this country—that the top five percent of the population have twenty percent of the wealth, and the bottom twenty percent have five percent of the wealth, or whatever the figures are. But this is perfectly normal, and justifiable. For wealth is

affected by many factors not controllable by the state. No matter what laws we passed, we could not prevent there being some disparity between the better-off and the worse-off people.

5. The company conceded that it had no good reason for changing the shift periods; in other words, its action was arbitrary. That is why the union is strongly opposing the change, for how can we bow to arbitrary and capricious company decisions, since an arbitrary decision is one taken despite good reasons to the contrary?

EXERCISE 5C

Make up five ambiguous sentences. Disambiguate each one by rewriting it in different ways. Select one of the ambiguities and construct an argument in which there is equivocation on the two meanings.

EXERCISE 5D

The following passage contains some key words and phrases that are somewhat ambiguous or vague. Decide what you think they ought to mean in this context, and rewrite the passage so as to eliminate the ambiguity and reduce the vagueness.

It is my firm belief that President Nixon should never have resigned from the presidency. When General Haig urged him to resign, he believed that a Senate vote of conviction on the impeachment was certain; but this was only his opinion, not his hope. The Senate might not have sustained it. The Nixon foes were out to get him, and the chips were down. Leaders of the media were at best disinterested in his case, and at worst unwilling to be loyal to the presidency in its hour of peril. Surely there were obstacles. Nevertheless, the President's horoscope remained as favorable as ever; the signs were positive, the way was clear. If he had stayed in office and stuck to his story, he was bound to win.

PULLING OUT THE STOPS

emotive language

Words are emotive in two ways: as expressive and as evocative. A word *expresses* emotion when the use of it, at least in that context, tends to show how the writer feels about whatever it is he is applying the word to. A word *evokes* emotion when the use of it, in that context, tends to arouse certain feelings in those who are likely to read it. (As always in this book, what I say about writing applies also to speaking, and what I say about reading applies also to hearing.)

The word "tends," or some other qualification, is needed in these definitions because the connection between word and feeling is not universal. To call a man a "fairy" is not only to say that he is a homosexual, but also to express contempt, or at least aversion; and anyone who uses the word while aware of its emotive expressiveness will in fact have the feelings he expresses. But someone who is not very much at home in the English language might use the word without realizing that it expresses contempt; so in using it, he would be expressing contempt, even though he himself does not feel that way at all. On the other side, to call someone a "solid citizen and one hundred percent American" is likely to stir up warm feelings toward that person in the minds of those to whom the remark is addressed. It will not necessarily move everyone who hears it; some may even be turned off by so blatant an appeal to their feelings. Still, we can recognize this phrase as emotively evocative, speaking broadly; and anyone who uses it probably intends to produce those emotive effects.

Emotive expressiveness and emotive evocativeness often go hand in hand: words that express anger, pity, fear, affection, respect are likely to evoke anger, pity, fear, affection, respect. Still, the two kinds of emotiveness should be kept distinct. And they do not always coincide: words that express annoyance, jealousy, greed, envy will seldom arouse these same feelings in those who hear them. They may arouse quite different feelings, or none at all.

Language arouses feelings through what it means and what it says. If "fink" and "phony" are negative—are deprecatory or condemnatory words—that is in large part because of the nature of finks and phonies, or at least because of what is generally believed to be true about them. If the housing development for retired people is called "Golden Years Leisure Village," it is because these carefully chosen positive words— laudatory and praising—are understood to imply certain things about that development. Of course, the description may be a kind of lie, or may be only half-believed by those who hand over their life savings to the manager. Still, the warm glow of approval and the inclination to sign up are produced through an understanding of what the words mean and of what assertion is (at least implicitly) being made. Sentences can be both emotive and true.

Thus, there is no inherent conflict between the emotive aspect of emotive language (its expressiveness and evocativeness) and its logical aspect (its meaning and its truth or falsity). Consider this argument:

> The police have raided the premises of the local chapter of the Jewish Defense League and seized its records, without obtaining a warrant by a show of "probable cause." Such entry is unconstitutional. Hence, the police have acted unconstitutionally.

One would expect such an argument to be made in a good deal less restrained manner; indeed, it is hard to see how anyone could wish to offer this argument unless he felt a certain amount of moral indignation about such a flagrant violation of civil liberties. If he feels that strongly about the matter and if his indignation is perfectly justified, why should he not feel free to share it with others? So we get something like this:

> The local storm troopers of our police department deserve the strongest condemnation for their latest gross violation of civil liberties. By entering the premises of the Jewish Defense League and seizing its records, without obtaining a warrant (which would require them to show "probable cause" that a crime had been or would be committed), these neo-Nazis have trampled on the Constitution and on individual rights.

The logical argument is still here, just as good as it was before. The arguer, though worked up, has not lost track of what he is arguing for, and his feeling have not led him to equivocate or miss the point. The expression of emotions, then, need not interfere with thought or weaken it logically, when the emotions grow naturally and ethically out of the ideas themselves, and are kept under control by those ideas.

But, of course—and this is a matter we shall return to shortly—emotions can get in the way. One who is aroused will often be somewhat less scrupulous in the way he argues, a little less alert to the logical mistakes committed by himself or others. He may want too much to win his point, to make others feel the way he does, and he may be tempted to play on their feelings with emotive language rather than convince them with good reasons. So we get the kind of argument we are all too familiar with in political diatribes and advertising copy—lots of emotive language, backed up by few solid facts. Nothing leaves your argument more deflated than a reader who sees through the ranting and finds that under the surface the argument is hollow.

Even our arguer above, though he does not rant and he does give us a genuine argument, is not free from fault in his use of emotive language. Calling the police "storm troopers" and "neo-Nazis" is (to put it calmly) something of an overstatement. "Their latest gross violation" suggests that this has been done before, but the writer gives us no evidence of previous violations, and so to characterize the police as "storm troopers" (as though this were their usual procedure) is not warranted by anything provided in the argument. Emotive language always tempts us toward exaggeration and oversimplification of complex issues (such as, in this case, whether there may have been some special reason why a warrant was not obtainable or not required). This is the *abuse* of emotive language: expressing and arousing feelings that are not fully justified by the facts and inferences presented.

The lesson is to use emotive language, but mistrust it. This means, first, that you must be free to express such feelings as your outrage against injustice, your love of nature or of city life, your distress at the way your government may be functioning, your strong desire that a traffic light be installed at the corner near the school, where children have been injured by cars. But, second, you should make sure that you give the reasons that account for, and justify, these feelings—that the injustice really did occur, that the traffic light will not be merely a gesture but will actually remedy the situation. And, third, when you still have qualms, and are honestly concerned to make your argument as good as possible, but feel very strongly about something, you can protect yourself by deliberately toning down your language. Choose more *neutral* words to replace the emotive ones. See how the argument looks when you simply call the police "police" rather than unpleasant names and write of "acting unconstitutionally" rather than "trampling on the Constitution." Sometimes the only way you can be sure that you have a good argument is to strip it of emotive language, or at least of the most extreme emotive language, and look at it cold. If it still holds up, you can begin to let your feelings show—with due care and caution.

EXERCISE 6A

Try toning down the passage below by substituting more neutral words for those underlined.

When the Governor was <u>cavorting about</u> trying to get elected, and <u>snuggling up</u> to the voters with <u>cozy</u> promises of all that <u>pie in the sky</u> he was going to bring us, one of his <u>theme songs,</u> a haunting refrain, was "No income tax. No new taxes." We believed him, <u>brainwashed</u> as we were. Now he has been in office for three months, a <u>do-nothing</u> three months, and he has decided to make his move: he wants a state income tax, and he wants it now.

The Governor <u>complains</u> that he lacks funds to carry out essential state services. Well, we lack funds to pay the grocery bill. He constantly <u>mutters</u> that an increase in sales tax would unfairly hurt the poor—as though the middle class were not <u>drowning in taxes</u> already. He says he needs funds for mental hospitals, but what about the sane people who <u>slave away</u> at their jobs day after day?

When you take up the task of proving a thesis, you often find that you must not only give reasons for that thesis, you must also show why the reasons alleged against it are unsatisfactory. And this is especially so when the view you are rejecting has been defended with much passion and is widely clung to. It may not be enough merely to show (if you can show) that the arguments are specious and full of logical faults. You may have to get inside the opposing view, so to speak, and help people understand how anyone could have come to accept so illogical a conclusion. You may have to expose the maneuvers that have been used to conceal the weakness of the case—especially when the maneuvers have consisted in using emotive language to arouse desired feelings as a substitute for giving good reasons.

There is a danger here of your committing your own logical error, if you go too far.

> My opponent has defended his view with sleazy rhetoric and cheap emotional appeals—his intention is obviously to cover up the deficiencies of his argument. So it is obvious that his conclusion is false.

This attack is itself a kind of emotive appeal; it seeks to discredit the opponent's argument by casting aspersion on his motives. It has a name: the *ad hominem argument*—that is, an attack on the person, rather than on the merits of his view. Your opponent may be dishonest, disreputable, devious, and unkind to dogs. If you point out these things, no doubt some of your readers will lose confidence in what he says; there will be a credibility gap. But this is beside the point; it is an unfair form of disputation. Granted all these personal failings, still your opponent's argument may be a good one and his conclusion may be sound. The risk you run is that you may win an easy debating victory over him and come to think that you have really shown his view to be mistaken—when in fact you have only diverted attention (that of others, and even your own) from the argument to the arguer, and failed to meet the argument head on. An *ad hominem* argument, then, is one that attacks the person and claims to have weakened his case thereby. It is a dodge, and has no logical force.

Yet even if you cannot show an opponent's thesis to be false by questioning his motives or his character, you can legitimately show that it is but weakly or even negligibly supported by exposing your opponent's illegitimate strategies of persuasion. For suppose he is not committed to logical methods: he aims not to convince by reasons, but only to get people to agree with what he says and act as he wishes them to act. Then if you can show that there is little or nothing to his argument in the way of logical force, but only a huge smoke screen of emotional appeal, you have made a valuable strategic point. So it is useful to have in mind some of the commonest emotional appeals and to keep an eye out for their use. Six of them are especially frequent, and are worth noting.

1. Appeal to pride.

Welcome to all you good people—sons and daughters of the true silent majority, the great middle class that made this country great! I am sure you will agree with me when I say that . . .

This is flattery—not very subtle, to be sure. Perhaps it will soften up the audience so that they will be just a bit more open to the speaker's message. Of course, it might be true that the middle class made the country great, but whether it is true or not has no logical bearing on what is to come; it is just a way of arousing friendly and receptive feelings. And sometimes the only way to counter is to point out to the audience how they are being manipulated, and what contempt for their intelligence is implied in the speaker's assumption that he can con them so easily.

2. Appeal to fear.

I tell you, with all the solemnity I can express, that these days of two-digit inflation are days of darkness—not the darkness before the dawn, but the darkness before even greater darkness, as all our economic institutions (can you imagine the horror of it?), banks, corporations, the Federal Reserve System, the government itself, collapse under the pressures of constantly rising inflation and the decline in the value of money. Remember Germany before Hitler— ten million marks for a single sausage!

Now there is nothing illogical about pointing out real dangers, showing that they are indeed real and imminent, and trying to arouse people to that healthy fear that may galvanize them into constructive action. What is illegitimate is the evocation of a general panic that is not based on any serious argument (the speaker does not actually show that inflation will destroy banks, or that the situation is analogous to German inflation in the 1920s). If the audience is scared enough it may accept any proposal that is alleged to solve the problem—without looking closely enough at the nature and consequences of that proposal.

3. Appeal to pity.

The little girl pictured above is always hungry; she has never had enough to eat. Her parents work whenever they can to obtain a little food, but in the poor soil of the arid land where she lives, little can grow and there is no one to bring food or water. Won't you help this child by contributing to . . . ?

If we have good reason to believe that there is a genuine need for help and that the organization to which we contribute will use our money to give that help, there is certainly nothing objectionable in this appeal to pity. Pity is exactly what is called for. And when we turn our eyes and look about the world, we can find all too many real occasions for such pity and for charity. The logical danger arises when the appeal to pity is used to dull our critical faculties: to solicit funds for fake philanthropy (sometimes the "summer camps for poor children" that door-to-door solicitors with impressive papers claim to be helping exist only in the minds of con artists). If we are so filled with pity that we forget to consider the reality of the need and the reliability of the organization, we are the victims of an illegitimate appeal to pity.

4. *Appeal to respect.*

The safety and efficacy of this miracle drug has been attested to by the National Council of Ethical Drug Company Research.

It is always in order to support a conclusion by saying that it is accepted by a genuine authority in the area of knowledge to which the conclusion applies: the words of a qualified expert in medical research might well lend weight to an assertion about a drug. On the other hand, if the impressively named National Council is really a group of advertising copywriters who set up their organization to give a deceptive scientific air to their advertising copy, we have an appeal to *illegitimate authority*. As always, we must try to give our respect where respect is due, and not be carried away by big names and impressive titles.

5. *Appeal to inertia.*

We do not need your criticisms or suggestions. The way we run the shop here is the way it has always been run, since old J.G. started it. What was good enough in the past is good enough for me.

This is the "graybeard" argument: what has been done should continue to be done—not because it can be shown by other reasons to be the best way, but just because it has always been that way. Such an argument has little logical force; if Congress has for decades insisted on extremely inefficient and undemocratic ways of operating, that shows, perhaps, that at least the old ways were not so bad as to be utterly crippling, but it does not show that reform is undesirable.

6. Appeal to restlessness.

This is the New Way of getting your floors clean and shiny; throw out your old methods and cleaning implements. Start the New Way tomorrow!

Those who are left unmoved by the graybeard argument, which takes all change to be suspect, may be moved by the appeal to novelty, which takes all change to be welcome. Again, what is new will often be better, but the fact that it is new does not prove that it is better: if it is indeed better, that will have to be shown by more solid evidence.

EXERCISE 6B

How would you describe the emotive appeals in the following passages? What questions would you want to ask before deciding whether they are legitimate?

1. Hurry up, before you're too late! There are only a few of these beautiful pieces of Florida real estate left at these fantastically low prices. You will lose out unless you act at once! Do not delay! Send us your $1000 down payment, and Paradise is yours!

2. Dr. Manfred Micheljohn is prepared to enroll you in his widely admired Correspondence Course and Home Manual of Sexual Therapy. You pay only $75 for the entire course, which is guaranteed to resolve all your sexual problems and rid you of all hang-ups. Dr. Micheljohn has a Ph.D. in cellular biology, and is therefore an authority on living things and on life.

3. I don't care how many oddball ideas the students come up with for grading each others' papers or the courses themselves or even their teachers. I see no reason to alter time-tested and established procedures, by which the instructor gives his exams and grades them and rates the students from A to E in accord with his expert judgment.

4. I'm sure you will not be taken in by my opponent's feeble arguments. He tries hard, but he does not realize he is addressing a highly intelligent audience that is too sophisticated and clever to be fooled by specious arguments and sophistic debating tricks.

5. I'm so distressed by the treatment of the migrant workers! They are forced to live in unbelievably poor conditions, are at the mercy of their employers, and often earn very little for backbreaking work in the sun. Something must be done! The whole thing is a blot on America and a reproach to all of us. That is why I have proposed

to abolish the whole thing—no more migrant workers. If we make the practice illegal, we can end all of the abuses at once.

EXERCISE 6C

Select a newspaper editorial or newspaper column that you consider to be quite reasonable and emotionally neutral. Rewrite it in highly toned emotive language, introducing some emotional appeals. Notice how these changes tempt, or even require, you to make claims that go beyond what can be supported by the reasons at hand.

EXERCISE 6D

Select several of the words that are given in Roget's Thesaurus (an abridged edition will serve), along with lists of approximate synonyms. Classify the synonyms as (1) favorable, (2) unfavorable, or (3) neutral. What, if anything, does your little investigation suggest about the kinds of words that are likely to have fairly emotive synonyms and those that are not so likely to?

7

SAY IT IS — OR ISN'T — SO

logical incompatibility

What makes disputes possible, life interesting, and logic worth studying is a pervasive feature of propositions: their capacity to enter into logical opposition. Smith's assertion of proposition P runs into conflict with Jones's assertion of proposition Q when it turns out that P and Q cannot both be true.

> *Smith:* Orders to wiretap private citizens were at no time given by the White House, except in cases of national security where no danger of invasion of privacy existed.
>
> *Jones:* No: some private citizens whose privacy was in danger of being violated were subjected to wiretaps on orders from the White House, despite the absence of any danger to national security.

One might perhaps make something of the one verbal difference here—between "invasion" and "violation" of privacy—but it does not appear to be material. So the two propositions do conflict. They cannot both be true.

Two propositions that cannot both be true are *logically incompatible*. If either is true, the other must be false. To assert both of them is to fall into (logical) *inconsistency*.

Now suppose we have two propositions, R and S, that are logically incompatible with respect to their truth but also with respect to their falsity: it is impossible for both to be true, and it is impossible for both to be false. To put it another way, at least one of them must be true, and at least one of them must be false. Then R and S are *contradictories;* and if Smith asserts R and Jones asserts S, then Smith and Jones are contradicting each other. Moreover, if Smith himself asserts both R and S on the same occasion, he is contradicting himself. (I say "on the same occasion" because he might, after all, change his mind.)

The plainest contradictions are those obtained by *negating* a proposition. As we saw earlier, this can often be done by inserting "not" at the right place:

> Washington crossed the Delaware.
>
> Washington did not cross the Delaware.

Contradictories

Compound propositions are sometimes a little trickier to contradict exactly. Take, for example, a conditional proposition; it won't do just to negate its consequent:

> If Jones recommends Smith for the job, I will hire him.
>
> If Jones recommends Smith for the job, I will *not* hire him.

NOT contradictories

Here the second proposition makes it sound as though Jones's recommendation is the kiss of death. You have to put the negation more carefully:

> If Jones recommends Smith for the job, I will hire him.
>
> Even if Jones recommends Smith for the job, I still won't hire him.

Contradictories

Here, the second proposition simply says that Jones's recommendation will not suffice.

Some of the most interesting and useful contradictories are found among propositions of a certain kind that we now need to consider. Propositions about relations among classes (such as we used earlier in talking about classification) can be called *class propositions*. Conditional propositions are not class propositions, for they connect, not classes, but other propositions. Here, we shall be concerned with those class propositions that involve exactly two classes: call them *two-class propositions*.

Suppose the following two propositions are true about your city council:

A. All city council members are men.
B. No city council members are pediatricians.

Proposition A says that the class {city council members} is wholly included in the class {men}. Since class-inclusion propositions, such as this one, are most naturally expressed in affirmative sentences, let us call them *affirmative propositions* ("Cats are mammals"). Proposition B, on the other hand, says that the class {City Council members} is wholly excluded from the class {pediatricians}. Since class-exclusion propositions, such as this one, are most naturally expressed in negative sentences, let us call them *negative propositions* ("Cats are not dogs").

An equally basic distinction cuts across the distinction between affirmative and negative propositions. The two propositions above clearly apply to the entire class {city council members}. These are *universal propositions*. The inclusion or exclusion is complete. Other propositions are true of part of a class; in them, the inclusion or exclusion is *not* complete.

C. Some members of city council favor a sales tax.
D. Some members of city council do *not* favor a sales tax.

These are called *particular propositions*. Proposition C is affirmative, since it says that the class {city council members} is (at least) partly included in the class {people who favor a sales tax}. Proposition D is negative, since it says that the class {city council members} is (at least) partly excluded from the class {people who favor a sales tax}. Using A, B, C, and so on, as abbreviated names of classes, < for "is included in," and ⊀ for "is excluded from," we may list our four types of proposition as follows:

> ### The types of two-class proposition
>
> | | |
> |---|---|
> | All A < B | Universal Affirmative |
> | All A ≮ B | Universal Negative |
> | Some A < B | Particular Affirmative |
> | Some A ≮ B | Particular Negative |

It is not hard to find the contradictory pairs among these four types. It would be rather hard to put all the potatoes in the basket and at the same time leave some of them outside. It would be equally hard to keep all the flies out of the house while allowing some to remain inside. These are logical impossibilities, like square circles, four-sided triangles, married bachelors, and persons who know only one thing—namely, that they know nothing.

> ### Contradictories
>
> All A < B ———————————— All A ≮ B
> Some A < B ———————————— Some A ≮ B

The crossed lines indicate the contradictions: the universal affirmative and the particular negative are contradictories (when they have the same terms in the same order); the universal negative and the particular affirmative are contradictories (under the same condition). What, after all, could be plainer: *either* everyone likes parsnips *or* some don't, and it can't be that everyone likes parsnips *and* some don't; *either* no one likes parsnips *or* some do, and it can't be that no one likes parsnips *and* some do.

When you argue, you are affirming a conclusion; and this is the same as denying the contradictory of the conclusion. You are also attempting to prove the conclusion; and this is the same as attempting to refute the contradictory of the conclusion. Arguments often divide into two parts along these lines: you offer positive reasons to support your conclusion; you offer other reasons to show why you think your opponent's view is mistaken. The essential thing is to make sure you know what you are doing—that the proposition you are attacking is in fact the contradictory of the proposition you are defending.

But there is an even more important reason for knowing how to tell when two propositions are contradictory and when they are not: you don't want to contradict yourself. An editorial writer says:

> Research has amply demonstrated the futility as well as the cruelty of capital punishment: there is simply no evidence that it deters crime (any more than hanging pickpockets did in the eighteenth century: the pickpockets did their best business at the public hangings). There are essentially two types of criminals: passionate and professional. Those who act from passion are not deterred by the death threat because they are carried away by jealousy, fear, or whatever; the professionals always bet that they will evade arrest or beat the rap. So the bill to abolish capital punishment that is now before the legislature should be passed—and especially because it contains a very valuable protective feature, retaining the death penalty for crimes committed against policemen; for this will discourage attacks against them.

This passage says, on the one hand, that

> The death penalty does not deter any crimes,

and, on the other hand, that

> The death penalty does deter ("discourage") attacks on policemen.

Here is a real contradiction: capital punishment never deters, capital punishment sometimes deters. To write like this is to take away in one breath what has been said in another; it shows that the writer is deeply confused in his thinking. And such an editorial is not likely to be convincing to a thinking reader.

EXERCISE 7A

Which of the following pairs of propositions are contradictories?

1. (a) Bobby Fisher is the greatest chess player.
   (b) Other chess players are greater than Bobby Fisher.

2. (a) Bobby Fisher is the greatest chess player.
   (b) Other chess players are at least as great as Bobby Fisher.

3. (a) The runner was safe at first.
   (b) The runner was not safe at first.

4. (a) Good intentions never justify bad actions.
   (b) There are bad actions that are justified by good intentions.

5. (a) If Napoleon had won the Battle of Waterloo, he would have become emperor of France again.
   (b) If Napoleon had won the Battle of Waterloo, he would have become president of France.

6. (a) Smith and Jones are both going to run in the primary.
   (b) Neither Smith nor Jones is going to run in the primary.

7. (a) There is no point in continuing to negotiate.
   (b) There is some point in continuing to negotiate.

8. (a) Successful politicians are always gregarious.
   (b) Not every successful politician is gregarious.

9. (a) It will rain tomorrow.
   (b) It will snow tomororw.

10. (a) The price of oil will be higher next January first.
    (b) The price of oil will be lower next January first.

Contradictory propositions are logically opposed to each other in the sharpest possible way: they are diametrically opposed. But there is another kind of logical opposition that is also noteworthy, not only because it plays an important part in much of our reasoning, but also because it must be kept distinct from contradiction. Suppose two propositions, *P* and *Q*, are logically incompatible, but are *not* contradictories: that is, they cannot both be true, but they *could* both be false. Then they are *contraries* of each other.

Consider our fourfold classification of two-class propositions again, and this time the relationship between the universal affirmative and the universal negative proposition.

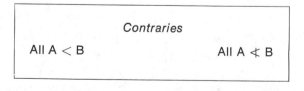

As we know, some people like parsnips, some do not. So it is not true that the class of human beings is wholly included in the class of parsnip likers; and it is not true that the class of human beings is wholly excluded from the class of parsnip likers. But it also can't be true that all human beings both like and dislike parsnips. So,

Everyone likes parsnips

and

No one likes parsnips

are contraries.

Any two propositions that can't both be true and yet leave open other possible alternatives are contraries. Compare:

The barn is entirely red. ⎤
                  Contraries
The barn is entirely white. ⎦

Possible alternatives are that the barn might be entirely blue, or partly red and partly white.

The soup is hot. ⎤
         Contraries
The soup is cold. ⎦

A possible alternative is that the soup might be lukewarm. That we can think of these logical alternatives shows each pair to be contraries, not contradictories.

Compound propositions can have their contraries too.

It will rain tonight and it will thunder tonight. ⎤
              Contraries
It will neither rain tonight nor thunder tonight. ⎦

Why aren't these contradictories? Well, could they both be false? Sure: it might rain but not thunder, or it might thunder but not rain. In either case, both propositions would be false. If you want strict contradictories, you have to say:

It will rain tonight and it will thunder tonight. ⎤
              Contradictories
It will either not rain tonight or not thunder tonight. ⎦

Two mistakes about contraries are commonly made. They are fatal to any argument, discussion, or dispute in which they turn up. One consists in confusing contraries with contradictories. The other consists in thinking that two propositions are incompatible when they are really not.

The first mistake has perhaps been emphasized enough already; but a few more remarks may not be amiss. When you think you are contradicting someone, offering Q as a contradictory of P, you have to make sure that there is no third (or fourth, or fifth ...) alternative. Otherwise, you may think that in refuting your opponent's view you have automatically proved your own—which you have, *if* (and only if) the two views are genuine contradictories.

The second mistake is easy to spot with simple examples.

> *Smith:* Some federal government officials are corrupt.
> *Jones:* Absurd! The fact is that some state and local government officials are corrupt.

This little exchange is not likely to occur unless passions are high and the parties are confused. If Jones thinks he is contradicting Smith, he is badly mistaken.

> *Smith:* This tabletop is square.
> *Jones:* No, this tabletop is rectangular.

Perhaps Jones is overeager to pick a fight with Smith, or perhaps he doesn't have a clear idea of what a rectangle is. He seems to think he is denying what Smith said, but of course he is not. For a square is one sort of rectangle (in that all four of its angles are right angles), so Jones's proposition is perfectly consistent with Smith's. There is no real dispute.

Fake contrariety, or the illusion of incompatibility, may be harder to avoid, or to detect, in more elaborate disputes.

> *Smith:* If President Kennedy had not been assassinated, he would have restrained the country's deepening involvement in Southeast Asia, and we would never have had the agony and the catastrophe of the Vietnam War.
> *Jones:* On the contrary: if President Kennedy had lived out his term, he would never have been able to carry through the desperately needed social reforms in this country that President Johnson was able to push through Congress—such as the war on poverty.

Now any dispute over a subject so broad and profound as this is not to be summed up in a simple formula. It may be that what Smith says is part of a general defense of some such thesis as:

If President Kennedy had not been assassinated, the country would have been better off. (Smith's thesis?)

And it may be that what Jones has in mind is the claim that:

If President Kennedy had not been assassinated, the country would have been worse off—or at least not better off. (Jones's thesis?)

In that case, there would be a genuine incompatibility. But this is guesswork. What they actually say is something more limited:

Smith: If President Kennedy had not been assassinated, we would not have become involved in the war.
Jones: If President Kennedy had not been assassinated, domestic problems would not have been dealt with.

And these two propositions do not (logically) conflict. We have not a dispute, but a pseudo dispute. The way to avoid it is to be clear about the nature of logical opposition.

EXERCISE 7B

Which of the following pairs of propositions are contraries?

1. (a) Most people who chew gum are tense persons.
   (b) Most people who chew gum are relaxed persons.

2. (a) Jones was in Boston at noon on Independence Day, 1974.
   (b) Jones was in Philadelphia at noon on Independence Day, 1974.

3. (a) Every member of the club has paid his dues.
   (b) Not every member of the club has paid his dues.

4. (a) George Washington was a soldier.
   (b) George Washington was a soldier *and* a statesman.

5. (a) That tree is deciduous.
   (b) That tree is very old.

6. (a) Few barking dogs bite.
   (b) Many barking dogs bite.

7. (a) Sunday evening's concert by the Philharmonic will be an all-Beethoven program.
   (b) Sunday evening's concert by the Philharmonic will be an all-Mozart program.

8. (a) Unhappy people are always unpopular.
   (b) Unpopular people are always unhappy.

9. (a) Only Ph.D.'s make competent college teachers.
   (b) Only persons who are not Ph.D.'s make competent college teachers.

10. (a) A good way to get to New Jersey is over the Ben Franklin Bridge.
    (b) A good way to get to New Jersey is over the Walt Whitman Bridge.

EXERCISE 7C

Find two newspaper editorials or newspaper columns that take different sides on an issue currently under dispute. (They might be for and against a particular tax, strip mining, sex education in public schools, increased military expenditures, legalizing marijuana.) Analyze the logical clashes between the two arguments: At what points do they contradict each other? At what points are their propositions contrary to each other?

EXERCISE 7D

Suppose the Administration of your college has made the following three statements about college financial policy:

1. All student tuitions should be raised $200.

2. Some Administration salaries should be raised by small amounts.

3. No faculty salaries should be raised.

Write a letter to the editor of the college newspaper arguing briefly against these three propositions, that is, supporting their contradictories.

8

WHAT FOLLOWS?

logical implication

When you run across a proposition that seems to be a significant one, you may stop and think about it. You want to know not only what it *is*, but what else can legitimately be inferred from it. You wonder: what follows? And the same is true of your own propositions when you are trying to say something significant to others: you should be aware not only of what you are directly and explicitly saying, but also of what you may be logically implying by what you say.

Generally, not very much follows from a single proposition. But when several propositions are combined in an argument, they may become a powerful and convincing reason for accepting a conclusion. Such arguments will engage our attention shortly. But first, it is well to familiarize ourselves with the basic logical connections among propositions—connections that can hold for single propositions as well as for groups. These are best brought out by comparatively simple examples.

The notion of one proposition's following (logically) from another is very fundamental in logic, but it is not definable in any simple way. We can give more or less synonymous descriptions: if one proposition is true, then it constitutes a good reason for believing the other one; one proposition lends some degree of support to the other, so that a rational person would be justified in accepting the second proposition if he already accepted the first one. Conversely, anyone who accepted the first proposition but refused to accept the second would (in the absence of further reasons he might advance) be acting in an irrational fashion. When proposition Q follows logically from proposition P, this does not mean that believing P actually leads people to believe Q—that is, to make the inference. It means that the inference is actually warranted: knowing that P is true gives us the *right* to believe Q, because the truth of P gives us some assurance that Q is also true.

So much can be said in general about logical following. Yet a distinction must be made. Logical following appears in two very different patterns, which must never be confused. They correspond to two basic forms of inference: *probable inference* and *necessary inference*. Consider the following claims:

> George is wearing a Phi Beta Kappa key. *It follows that* George is a member of Phi Beta Kappa.
> John is performing an operation, removing someone's appendix. *It follows that* John is a surgeon.
> Henry is standing in court wearing a policeman's uniform. *It follows that* Henry is a police officer.

I guess we would all agree that these are pretty good inferences—not only psychologically natural, but logically warranted. Anyone who went around refusing to make such inferences would seem rather odd, and would end up knowing a lot less than the rest of us.

But note that some risk is involved, even in these plain cases. George *might* have stolen someone else's Phi Beta Kappa key. John might be an imposter, who somehow fooled people into thinking he had gone to medical school (such cases have happened). Henry may be impersonating a police officer, for a nefarious purpose of his own. We cannot be *certain* that Henry is a police officer, even if we are certain that he is standing in court wearing a policeman's uniform. The inference has the form, then, of a probability inference: P is so; it *follows probably* that Q is so. The probability may be extremely high, which makes the inference a good one; but it is still probability.

Probable inference (which is inductive inference, or *induction*) is an essential source of much of our knowledge. What we know about the chemical composition of the moon, about the guilt or innocence of defendants in court, about the greatness of certain poets or musicians, about the rate of inflation next year, is based on probable inference. So we shall return to this topic in Chapters 11–14. But those later discussions will be more satisfactory if we first consider, in this and the next few chapters, the second way in which one proposition can logically follow from another: that which justifies necessary inference.

Consider the following claims:

George has a dollar bill and six dimes in his pocket. *It follows that* George has money in his pocket.

The only operations that John has performed are appendectomies. *It follows that* all operations of other kinds have been performed by someone else.

Henry is the chief of police. *It follows that* any illegal acts committed by Henry were committed by the chief of police.

How do these differ from the examples above? First, it is obvious that they are far less risky. In the probable inferences, the conclusion went beyond what was given in the premise; in the necessary inferences, the conclusion tells us no more (and often less) than the premise. This is the secret of safety: what makes these inferences necessary ones is precisely that it is logically impossible for the premise to be true and the conclusion false. You cannot conceive of George's having dimes in his pocket without having money in his pocket. Dimes are (by definition) money; so to have dimes but not money would be a logical contradiction.

Q follows necessarily from *P*, then, if and only if it would be logically inconsistent to affirm *P* and deny *Q*. When you have hold of a necessary connection like this, you have the strongest possible connection between one proposition (or group of propositions) and another.

Of course, this does not mean that you can't make mistakes about necessary inference. If you aren't careful, and if the argument is complicated, you might fail to see that there is a necessary connection between *P* and *Q*. Suppose the dean's memorandum reads:

Not every student who has failed to appear for a term examination since the beginning of the semester will be denied permission not to make up the course.

Does this conclusion necessarily follow?

> Some students who will be given permission to omit making up the course are students who have failed to appear for a term examination since the beginning of the semester.

Maybe the answer is not immediately obvious. On the other hand, you might think that the conclusion follows necessarily when it really doesn't. This is what happens when you make a mistake in adding up your grocery list. If the items on the list are

$1.62
  .59
3.18
2.93
  .19
7.07
―――

then it follows necessarily that the sum is $15.58. But anyone might add the figures wrongly, especially if he were in a hurry. The point is that there is a specific figure that is the necessary sum of those figures— whether we know it or not.

When one proposition follows necessarily from another, the second one *logically implies* the first one. Logical implication is something quite special, and is not to be confused with other things that are also commonly called "implication." For example, if the host remarks to his late-staying guests that he has a hard day ahead tomorrow, he implies that it's time for them to leave—that is, his remark suggests that this is what he is thinking. But this is not logical implication (it could be called "rhetorical implication").

Necessary inference is deductive inference, or *deduction*.

A mathematical proof or calculation consists of nothing but necessary inferences, but ordinary prose passages very seldom aspire to this degree of rigor. Most of the inferences in familiar compositions are probable inferences. Nevertheless, most compositions contain some necessary inferences, and could not get along without them; that is, some of the crucial steps of reasoning depend on logical implications, and the whole argument would break down if these steps were not dependable. So when you argue, you have to know how much weight you can rest on your own inferences—whether it is barely credible, or quite likely, or completely certain that Q follows from P. If your reader is to know exactly how much confidence you place in your own inferences, so that he is not misled, then you must yourself be clear about whether your argument, or the particular step of your argument, is a necessary inference or a probable one—and, if a probable one, how probable it is.

EXERCISE 8A

Which of the following are probable inferences (P) and which are necessary inferences (N)? (The usual sign for "therefore" is used as an abbreviation for "it follows that.")

1. The sign in the window says "Help Wanted." ∴ Help is wanted.

2. The sky is red this evening. ∴ It will be a fine day tomorrow.

3. This egg was just laid. ∴ It is fresh.

4. This is a cookbook. ∴ It contains recipes.

5. That house is a national monument. ∴ The owner of that house is the owner of a national monument.

6. Albert is Benny's cousin. ∴ Benny is Albert's cousin.

7. A football field is rectangular. ∴ A football field has four sides.

8. Susan is eating voraciously. ∴ Susan is hungry.

9. Sam spent a day in Budapest. ∴ Sam speaks fluent Hungarian.

10. Sam can read Hungarian newspapers. ∴ Sam can read Hungarian philosophy.

Suppose two rival insurance salesmen are trying to persuade you to buy a policy. You read the fine print and discover that the only difference between the two policies is that one contains this sentence:

All policies are subject to cancellation for cause by the insuror except those for which the special noncancellation fee has been paid, as noted on the accompanying form.

And the other contains, instead, this sentence:

No policies for which the special noncancellation fee has not been paid, as noted on the accompanying form, are protected against cancellation for cause by the insuror.

Perhaps at first the second policy sounds a bit more discouraging, so you are inclined to buy the first policy. But the second salesmen assures you that there is no significant difference: his policy "says the same thing in different words"—it makes no logical difference (as he might better have said), because everything that follows from either of these propositions also follows from the other.

Is he right? Are they equally acceptable? Or would one of them, under some circumstances, cost you more or pay you less? Now of course the two sentences are not exactly alike—you might prefer the style of the first one, for example. But from a logical point of view we are concerned with other aspects. We want to know whether the two propositions are *logically equivalent;* for if they are, then it doesn't matter which policy you choose: exactly the same consequences will follow from both of them.

Two propositions are logically equivalent when each implies the other. This is a very intimate relationship. If you know that

No Republicans are on city council,

you can infer that

None of the members of city council is a Republican.

And vice versa. In more concise form (the double arrow stands for logical equivalence):

$$\text{All } R \nless C \qquad \longleftrightarrow \qquad \text{All } C \nless R$$

This equivalence is not trivial. One of the propositions tells you that if you ask every Republican in town, you'll discover that none is on city council; the other tells you that if you check with every member of city council, you'll discover that not one is a Republican. At least, if you were to complete either of these inquiries, you could see by *logic alone* that there is no need to undertake the other.

The equivalence just noted can be described by saying that universal negative propositions are *convertible:* if they are true in one direction they must be true in the other direction, and if they are false in one direction they must be false in the other direction. Switching the terms around will not affect their truth or falsity. The same is true of particular affirmative propositions:

Some railroads are bankrupt $\longleftrightarrow$ Some bankrupt businesses are railroads.

But the other two types of two-class propositions are not convertible at all. For example, the universal affirmative proposition,

Every virtuous person is happy,

neither implies nor is implied by

> Every happy person is virtuous.

And in exactly the same way, the particular negative proposition,

> Some virtuous persons are not happy,

and its converse,

> Some happy persons are not virtuous,

are *logically independent*—that is, the truth or falsity of one of them has no bearing upon the truth or falsity of the other.

A somewhat more striking and interesting form of equivalence appears when we compare two propositions that are related in the following ways: the second one negates the first one and at the same time negates its predicate. Start with:

> All skiers are daring.

First, change the proposition from affirmative to negative ("No skiers are daring"); second, change the predicate to its negative ("nondaring," or a synonymous term if you can think of a good one—that is, one appropriate to the context). The result:

> No skiers are nondaring—

which is equivalent to the original. Remember not to change the proposition from universal to particular, or vice versa, and not to negate the *subject* of the proposition. When we apply the same procedure to the other three types of two-class proposition, we obtain the following equivalences:

$$\text{All } A < B \longleftrightarrow \text{All } A \nless \text{non-B}$$
$$\text{Some } A < B \longleftrightarrow \text{Some } A \nless \text{non-B}$$
$$\text{All } A \nless B \longleftrightarrow \text{All } A < \text{non-B}$$
$$\text{Some } A \nless B \longleftrightarrow \text{Some } A < \text{non-B}$$

To get from propositions on the left side to propositions on the right side, we follow the procedure I have suggested. To get from the right side to the left, we do the same, but we must also take advantage of another familiar and fundamental logical principle: the principle of *double negation*. This simply states that non–non-B is the same as B.

There is one more two-class equivalence that is extremely useful in reasoning: it is the same principle we use, for example, when we figure that if all those who have worked in the United States have a Social Security number, then anyone without a Social Security number has never worked in the United States. Schematically:

All A $<$ B $\longleftrightarrow$ All non-B $<$ non-A

Like the other equivalences we have been taking note of, this one seems fairly innocuous by itself. Yet though it does not constitute a long leap of reasoning, we could not reason very far without it. The most complicated thoughts, in atomic physics as well as in the theory of literary criticism, are built of small but indispensable steps. And the secret of getting the whole right—of reasoning well and truly to sound conclusions —consists in making sure that the little steps of which it is composed proceed according to logical principles.

The principle we just noted has a close analogue for conditional propositions. Suppose it is true that *if* Jones is a professor, *then* he has a Ph.D. degree. It follows that if Jones does *not* have a Ph.D. degree, then he is *not* a professor. The inference proceeds both ways. Schematically:

If P then Q $\longleftrightarrow$ If not-Q then not-P

Of course, it doesn't follow that if Jones is not a professor, then he does not have a Ph.D. degree. For it could be the case that all professors are Ph.D.'s, but not all Ph.D.'s are professors.

One other pair of equivalences for compound propositions needs to engage our attention for a moment. These have to do with the relationship of "and" and "or." The denial of an and-proposition is always an or-proposition; the denial of an or-proposition is always an and-proposition. The equivalences work this way:

Not both P and Q $\longleftrightarrow$ Either not-P or not-Q
Not either P or Q $\longleftrightarrow$ Both not-P and not-Q

If you don't go to both the grocery store *and* the drug store today, that is the same as either not going to the grocery *or* not going to the drug store. If you don't buy *either* butter or margarine, that is the same as not buying butter *and* not buying margarine.

My aim in reviewing these elementary equivalences is not to

provide rules for memorization, but to help you become a little more self-conscious about the way you in fact reason when you are at your best. All the equivalences are quite obvious, once we state them. Yet we can make mistakes about them when we are in a hurry or when the verbal context is complicated and confusing. So they are worth attention. One of the more pathetic sorts of futility in writing comes when you are not quite sure what propositions are equivalent to the main thesis, or central conclusion, that you wish to defend. You find someone who seems to disagree with you, and you set about attacking his view with spirit— only to discover later on, when you have stopped to analyze, that in fact his view, though expressed in different words, is equivalent to your own. There is no real disagreement, and there is no call for mutual refutation.

EXERCISE 8B

Which of the following pairs of propositions are logically equivalent (E)? (It may be helpful to restate some of them as class inclusions or class exclusions.)

1. (a) Only the virtuous deserve to be happy.
    (b) Only those who deserve to be happy are virtuous.

2. (a) If he hadn't been a good driver, he wouldn't have escaped the collision.
    (b) If he escaped the collision, he was a good driver.

3. (a) Congress is not consulted on every executive agreement.
    (b) Not everything Congress is consulted on is an executive agreement.

4. (a) I'm sure I didn't order both the soup and the tomato juice.
    (b) I'm sure that I didn't order either the soup or the tomato juice.

5. (a) Nothing worthwhile is accomplished without effort.
    (b) Everything worthwhile is accomplished with some effort.

6. (a) Some of the toys you buy children these days are not durable.
    (b) Some of the nondurable things you buy these days are children's toys.

7. (a) He will vote for the incumbent if his mother does.
    He will not vote for the incumbent if his mother doesn't.

8. (a) Not every kind person is liked.
   (b) Not every unkind person is disliked.

9. (a) Martin's remarks are never witty.
   (b) Witty remarks are never made by Martin.

10. (a) Only expert typists use electric typewriters.
    (b) Expert typists use only electric typewriters.

EXERCISE 8C

Select a passage from a magazine or book, one that involves some argument, and rewrite it by substituting for each sentence, or clause, another one logically equivalent to it. Use the equivalences presented in this chapter and others that may occur to you. Now write a short essay discussing the differences in meaning between the two passages—that is, in style, in tone, in what they suggest about the writer and his attitude toward his subject and his reader—despite their basic logical equivalence.

9

SOME CLASSY ARGUMENTS

the syllogism

There is a simple kind of deductive argument that we all resort to constantly, whether or not we know its name: the *syllogism*. Its crucial role in our thinking is usually unnoticed. What distinguishes this form of argument from all others is that it involves (1) three two-class propositions, of which two are premises and one is the conclusion, and (2) three classes, each of which appears in exactly two of the propositions.

All selfish actions are morally dubious (actions).
Some selfish actions are kind (actions).
_____
Some kind actions are morally dubious (actions).

The premises are above, the conclusion below, the line (which can be read, "therefore"). The two premises together are the reason for the conclusion; the argument embodies a claim that the premises imply the conclusion. When the premises of a syllogism *do* imply its conclusion, the syllogism is *valid*.

Our task now is to get a grip on the nature of syllogisms: what makes them valid when they are valid, what makes them invalid when they are invalid. We must first give a general account of the basic strategies of syllogistic inference and of the various forms that syllogisms can take.

The first principle of the syllogism is that no conclusion can be drawn unless at least one premise is a universal proposition. A syllogism enables us to infer a relationship between two classes, A and C, from what we know about the relationship that each of them has to a third class, B. But somewhere along the line we must know something about the *whole* of at least one of the three classes, or the connections will not be strong enough to yield any conclusion. You might know that:

> Some credit-card holders are lawyers.
> Some lawyers are prosperous.

But these premises won't tell you anything about the relationship between the class ⎰credit-card holders⎱ and the class ⎰prosperous people⎱ .There is not enough information here to warrant a deductive inference. Now, if we knew that *all* lawyers are prosperous. . . . But we shall come to that in a moment.

At least one premise must be universal; and if only one is universal, it is the *major premise*. That is the one we shall put first, for convenience. If both premises are universal, it doesn't matter much which you put first. But here is a suggestion: look at the conclusion and see which class is referred to in its predicate. Call that the "major class." Then whichever premise refers to this class is the major premise. For example:

> Friends of Alec's are all enemies of Brit's, and therefore can't be friends of Carl's, because no friends of Carl's are enemies of Brit's.

This little syllogism is not particularly obscure. But to be perfectly clear about what it says, we can put it in proper form. The conclusion is "No friends of Alec's are *friends of Carl's*," so the class ⎰friends of Carl's⎱ is the major class (since it is referred to in the predicate of the conclusion). This major class is also referred to in one premise: "No *friends of Carl's* are enemies of Brit's"—so this premise is the major premise, and goes first:

No friends of Carl's are enemies of Brit's. ✓
All friends of Alec's are enemies of Brit's. ✓
_____
No friends of Alec's are friends of Carl's.

Since there are two kinds of universal proposition, affirmative and negative, we can divide all syllogisms into two basic groups: those with an affirmative major premise (let us call them "A-major syllogisms") and those with a negative major premise (let us call them "N-major syllogisms"). We shall consider A-major syllogisms first.

Suppose you have a true universal affirmative proposition available for use in constructing a syllogistic argument:

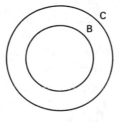

ALL B < C

What other information could you combine with this to allow a valid inference? Well, if you knew that some third class was wholly included in B, you could infer that it must also be wholly included in C. For, as the diagram makes plain, anything inside B must be inside C. So we try adding a second premise, which will be our *minor premise*, and the result looks like this:

All B < C
All A < B
_____
All A < C

For a real-life example, consider the following:

In taking office, presidents are always required to take an oath to ✓ see that the nation's laws are executed, and anyone who takes such an oath is subject to impeachment if he violates it; hence, every president is subject to impeachment if he violates his oath of office.

Here the premises are reversed, but we can spot the major premise well enough. In an A-major syllogism, the major premise is the premise that refers to the largest of the three classes in the syllogism. The class { presidents taking office } is said to be wholly included in the class { persons taking an oath to execute the laws } . And the class { persons taking such an oath } is said to be wholly included in the class { persons subject to impeachment for violating their oath } . So the class { persons subject to impeachment for violating their oath } is the largest class, and the second premise is the major premise:

All { persons who take an oath to execute the laws } < { persons who are subject to impeachment for violating their oath } . ✓

All { presidents taking office } < { persons who take an oath to execute the laws } .

All { presidents taking office } < { persons who are subject to impeachment for violating their oath } .

This argument would seldom be stated in so explicit a form as this, yet in its more natural form (above) it might play an important role in a discussion of constitutional law.

Given the universal affirmative premise, all B < C, then, we can draw a conclusion if we also know that all A < B. And this works just as well with a particular minor premise, some A < B—except that in this case, of course, the conclusion must be particular, too. If all A are B, then all A are C (given that all B are C); and if some A are B, then some A are C. So we have now discovered two forms of the A-major syllogism: (1) the kind with a universal affirmative minor premise and (2) the kind with a particular affirmative minor premise.

What other forms of syllogism are possible with our A-major premise? Look at the diagram on p. 87 again. Evidently, anything that happened to fall *outside* the C circle would have to fall outside the B circle too, since B is inside C. This suggests that we can draw a different sort of conclusion if we choose the right kind of *negative* minor premise —that is, a premise that excludes the class A from the class C.

All B < C
All A ≮ C

All A ≮ B

And this is also bound to work with the right kind of particular negative premise:

All B < C
Some A ≮ C

Some A ≮ B

So we have discovered two more forms of the A-major syllogism: (3) the kind with a universal negative minor premise and (4) the kind with a particular negative minor premise.

It seems that any of the four kinds of two-class proposition can be combined with a universal affirmative major premise to yield a valid syllogistic conclusion—you just have to make sure it has the right terms in the right places. And the basic idea can be stated in two very simple —though very powerful—principles:

> Whatever is included in a class is necessarily included in any class that class is included in.
> Whatever is excluded from a class is necessarily excluded from any class included in that class.

If these principles are a bit tongue-twisty, don't let that bother you: just think of the two nested circles and make up your own examples to help fix them in mind. For example:

> Whatever is inside your kitchen must be inside any area your kitchen is inside (such as the whole house).
> Whatever is outside your house must be outside any area that is inside your house (such as the kitchen).

Think of how you might take advantage of these truths in common-sense reasoning:

> Of course the stove is inside the house; it's in the kitchen, isn't it?
> Of course the shovel is not in the kitchen; it's in the garage.

We have now distinguished four forms of A-major syllogisms:

A–Major Syllogism Forms	
Type 1	Type 2
All B $<$ C	All B $<$ C
All A $<$ B	All A $\not<$ C
All A $<$ C	All A $\not<$ B
Type 3	Type 4
All B $<$ C	All B $<$ C
Some A $<$ B	Some A $\not<$ C
Some A $<$ C	Some A $\not<$ B

Here is an example of Type 2 as it might appear in an editorial or magazine article:

> A person is a being that possesses consciousness and the capacity to relate to other persons, but embryos do not satisfy this description —which is why it is an error to say that embryos are genuine persons.

This is not a suitable occasion to discuss the difficult—though important and interesting—issues about the nature of embryos and the justification of abortion. You may take exception at once to this argument and want to attack it; or you may accept it as a good one. But an important logical distinction is involved here, and this is the place to point it out. This argument is valid—which means that *if* both premises are true, *then* the conclusion must be true. Its validity is even more evident when we recast it in our artificial mold:

All $\{$ persons $\}$ $<$ $\{$ beings that possess consciousness and the capacity to relate to other persons $\}$.

All $\{$ embryos $\}$ $\nless$ $\{$ beings that possess consciousness and the capacity to relate to other persons $\}$.

All $\{$ embryos $\}$ $\nless$ $\{$ persons $\}$.

(One advantage of this technique of recasting the argument is that it helps us become more dispassionate and objective about it.)

When you confront a deductive argument, the first question is whether it is valid—and that is the question we are concerned with in the present chapter. The second question is whether the premises are true; that is a question we shall be concerned with in Chapters 11–14. Just knowing that the argument is valid is not enough to conclude that the conclusion is true; you also have to know that the premises are true. But supposing this argument to be valid (as I claim), then at least you know that if you wish to attack it, you must attack the truth of one or both of its premises. Our analysis of the argument even helps you here, because it brings out clearly the distinction between the two premises. The minor premise seems to be an empirical fact that could hardly be questioned: surely, embryos are not conscious. Therefore, an attack on the argument must focus on the concept of *person* that is formulated in the major premise. And this concept is, indeed, the focus of much of the debate about the morality of abortion.

We may turn now to the second basic type of syllogism: that in which the major premise is a universal negative proposition.

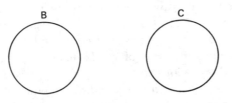

ALL B ⊀ C

What sorts of valid argument does this diagram suggest? Plainly, if we know that a third class, A, is included in B, we also know that it must be excluded from C; by the same token, if we know that A is included in C, we also know that A must be excluded from B. This gives us two slightly different syllogistic forms, each of which can be used with either a universal or a particular minor premise. So we have:

N–Major Syllogism Forms

Type 5	Type 6
All B ⊀ C	All B ⊀ C
All A < B	All A < C
All A ⊀ C	All A ⊀ B

Type 7	Type 8
All B ⊀ C	All B ⊀ C
Some A < B	Some A < C
Some A ⊀ C	Some A ⊀ B

After our discussion of A-major syllogisms, these forms are probably clear enough. They all rest on one basic principle:

Whatever is included in a class is necessarily excluded from any class excluded from that class.

Take two neighboring houses this time, each separated from the other on a typical suburban street. Since nothing can be inside both houses, the grand piano that is in one of the houses cannot possibly be in the other.

I don't want this brief treatment of N-major syllogisms to suggest that they are any less important than A-major syllogisms. They play an equally pervasive and indispensable role in our thinking. When the little league coach refuses to let girls play on his baseball team, and justifies his decision by citing a league rule that only boys may play in that league, he is thinking in terms of an N-major syllogism, of which the major premise is this obvious truth: no boys are girls. And whatever you may think of his decision, and of the rule (the minor premise) on which it is based, you can't fault the logic of his thinking.

There is one further variation on the syllogism that we need to take notice of, because it is so common and useful. Suppose the college registrar argues that according to his rules, no one with lower than a D average is allowed to remain in college, and Cyril has an average lower than D, so that Cyril is not allowed to remain in college. This argument is almost a syllogism, but it differs in one respect. The major premise is straightforward enough:

All $\left\{ \begin{array}{l} \text{students with a lower than D average} \end{array} \right\}$ ⊀ $\left\{ \begin{array}{l} \text{students allowed} \\ \text{to remain in college} \end{array} \right\}$.

But the minor premise is:

Cyril is a student with a lower than D average.

This is an affirmative proposition, but it is neither universal nor particular; it is in fact a *singular proposition*, because its subject, "Cyril," refers to a single individual. The minor premise, then, does not state a relationship between two classes, but between an individual (Cyril) and a class $\left\{ \begin{array}{l} \text{students with a lower than D average} \end{array} \right\}$. It says that Cyril is a member of this class.

Still, the inference is clearly valid, and we can bring it under our rules if we make one stipulation. Instead of thinking of Cyril, the individual, let us think of the class whose only member is Cyril. Classes can have just one member, just as they can have many members or no members; and Cyril, like everyone else, is in some class by himself (he is, for example, the only six-footer who lives in Room 221B of Baker Hall). So we can treat this argument as a syllogism after all. The class $\left\{ \begin{array}{l} \text{students with a lower than D average} \end{array} \right\}$ is excluded from the class $\left\{ \begin{array}{l} \text{students allowed to remain in college} \end{array} \right\}$. The class $\left\{ \begin{array}{l} \text{Cyril} \end{array} \right\}$ (that is, the class whose only member is Cyril) is included in the class $\left\{ \begin{array}{l} \text{students with a lower than D average} \end{array} \right\}$. And the conclusion follows validly. We have a syllogism of Type 5.

There is no special problem about negative singular propositions—we treat them as universal negatives. *1984* is the name of a novel, so any proposition of which it is the subject is a singular proposition. Hence, this syllogism of Type 2:

All $\{$novels by P. G. Wodehouse$\}$ $<$ $\{$funny (novels)$\}$. ✓
(All) $\{1984\}$ $\not<$ $\{$funny (novels)$\}$.
_____
(All) $\{1984\}$ $\not<$ $\{$novels by P. G. Wodehouse$\}$.

It is well to remind ourselves that the syllogisms that turn up in ordinary life, and that we ourselves are likely to frame when speaking or writing, are often casual and incomplete. If you write,

> Being a product of ghetto poverty, the Mayor of course understands the problems of the urban poor,

it will be clear enough, in most contexts, that you are presenting a syllogistic argument, though the major premise is omitted, and left for the reader to fill in for himself:

> (All persons brought up in ghetto poverty are persons who understand the problems of the urban poor.)

Sometimes these suppressed premises, or tacit assumptions, don't look as good when they are made explicit as they do when they are taken for granted and skipped over lightly. That's one of the reasons for stopping sometimes to make them explicit, thereby exposing the whole syllogism. But even when that's not necessary, we must keep an eye open for them, if we want to follow carefully all the steps of an argument. A syllogism condensed into a short sentence can zip by before you get a good look at it.

An argument, even a fairly elaborate one, may consist essentially of a syllogism, or series of syllogisms, with an extended defense of each premise and an expansive discussion or fuller explanation of the conclusion. Indeed, this is one of the firmest possible structures for an argument. When you are writing an essay in support of a certain conclusion, and beginning to think out the lines along which you will develop your support, you might do well to consider whether a syllogistic structure is not the most appropriate one. You may find that one of your premises is clear and uncontroversial, so that it needs hardly more than stating— but that the other premise requires a good deal more in the way of clarification and justification. Each premise may become the central point of its own paragraph, and you may present a third paragraph to draw and emphasize the conclusion. But that conclusion itself may become the premise of a second syllogism, built upon the first, if you can find another appropriate premise that will combine with it to yield still another conclusion. An argument constructed according to this pattern can be made easy for the reader to grasp, and if the reasoning is valid and each premise well established, the argument can also be very convincing.

EXERCISE 9A

Each of the following syllogistic arguments belongs to one of the eight forms that we have just distinguished. Recast each argument in terms of inclusion propositions and exclusion propositions, with the major premise first, and indicate its form by number.

1. John is an acrobat, so he must be daring; for acrobats are daring.

2. Some professional spies are not competent; for some get caught, and competent spies do not get caught.

3. There are poets who are obscure, and obscure writers are always admired; so some poets are admired.

4. Weddings are happy occasions, but not some family gatherings; hence, some family gatherings are not weddings.

5. Stringed instruments are beautiful, so viols must be, for viols are stringed instruments.

6. You can see that nothing permissible can be done to stop him; for only violence can stop him, and violence cannot be permitted.

7. There don't seem to be any unhappy bartenders; but there are bachelors who are bartenders and who must therefore not be unhappy.

8. Not everyone with parking stickers will find a place in the parking lot, but the faculty members will find a place; so there must be people with parking stickers who are not faculty members.

9. According to your testimony, the book you just finished is dull, but I know that books by John LeCarré are never dull; so I guess he didn't write that one.

10. No one who was present doubts the speaker's sincerity, but John does; evidently, he must not have been present.

We have discovered eight valid forms of the syllogism. The list is not complete: there are a few other forms, which can easily be obtained by converting the minor premises of the forms in our list. But our list will serve quite well for almost all purposes. The important thing is not to memorize the list but to bear in mind the basic reasoning involved in these relations among two-class propositions.

There is also an infinite variety of rhetorical variations on each of these syllogistic forms. Our list simply presents the skeletons of argument, not the living arguments themselves. Consider the following argument, which is of Type 4:

> Film masterpieces are characterized by expressive use of camera and of cutting, which, unfortunately, not all science-fiction movies have; it follows that there are science-fiction movies that are not masterpieces.

This argument could be presented in many different ways, depending on the context in which it is to fit. Compare the following version:

> Some science-fiction films are by no means masterpieces, as even their staunch defenders must concede when they reflect that some of these films are lacking in that expressive use of camera and cutting that is indispensable to a genuine masterpiece of cinematic art.

These two paragraphs present exactly the same syllogistic argument, but with different tones, styles, and rhetorical qualities; they express different attitudes and personalities in the writers. When you present an argument, even a fairly simple one, you have a complex task, because every word or phrase you choose, even the order in which you develop the argument (whether you put the conclusion first, or the major premise, or the minor premise), strongly affects the total meaning of what you write. In this book we are limited, however, to the logical point of view: our concern is not with these other important problems of composition, but only with the problem of getting the logic of the argument right.

For this purpose, we must consider not only the valid forms, but some of the commonest *invalid* forms, of the syllogism. You have to know what to avoid—what traps you might fall into—as well as what to do. And for this purpose, there are some general principles of validity that are worth noting and keeping in mind.

The first principle we have already noted: no conclusion can be drawn from the premises of a syllogism unless at least one of the premises is universal. The reasoning behind this principle was explained earlier. Any syllogism that violates it commits what we shall call Fault 1 (for syllogisms): *double particular*. This is just a handy label for syllogisms that are invalid because they have two particular premises.

There is an analogous fault for N-major syllogisms. Consider once more the diagram of the major premise:

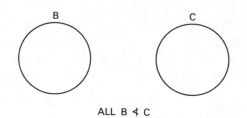

ALL B ⊀ C

We have seen that you can obtain a conclusion if the minor premise places some third class, or part of a class, inside one of the circles. Now someone might think that you could obtain a similar result if the minor premise placed the third class (or part of it) *outside* one of the circles. Such a mistake would lead to one or the other of the following invalid forms:

All B ⊀ C		All B ⊀ C	
All (some) A ⊀ B	✕	All (some) A ⊀ C	✕
All (some) A < C		All (some) A < B	

It's hard to see how anyone could make such a foolish mistake in reasoning while looking at the two separate circles. Imagine that the two circles contain all the cats and all the dogs, respectively. Of course, if you know that something is a cat, you know it's not a dog. But if you know it's *not* a cat, you obviously can't conclude that it *is* a dog. It might be a lemur or a yak. Yet this kind of mistake is not unknown.

> I grant that an innocent person would never conceal his knowledge about a crime, but this is precisely what supports my case. For my client, as he has testified (and his testimony has been confirmed by others) did not conceal his knowledge about the crime—which proves that he is innocent.

In more formal attire, the argument looks like this:

All {innocent persons} ⊀ {persons who would conceal knowledge about a crime} .

(All) {my client} ⊀ {persons who would conceal knowledge about a crime} .

───

(All) {my client} < {innocent persons} .

This is the second type of invalid argument sketched above.

The trouble with these invalid forms is clear enough when we inspect them: no conclusion can be drawn from two negative premises—that is, from two premises that are both exclusion propositions. At least one premise must be an inclusion. This is our second principle of syllogistic reasoning. And the corresponding Fault 2 is *double exclusion*.

Turn back now to the diagram of the A-major premise:

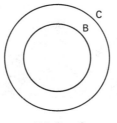

ALL B < C

As we have seen, if you were to put a dot inside B, you could be sure it would also be inside C; and if you put a dot outside C, you could be sure it would also be outside B. But what if you put the dot inside C? It might or might not be inside B. And if you put the dot outside B, it might or might not be outside C. So we have two other principles to consider.

The third principle of syllogistic reasoning is that in an A-major syllogism no conclusion can be drawn if the minor premise places the third class inside the outer circle (representing the major class). Hearing now from the prosecuting attorney:

> It is well known that guilty persons flee from the scene of a crime, which is exactly what the defendant did; it follows that the defendant is guilty.

This syllogism has the following form (using appropriate letters for "defendant," "guilty persons," and "fleeing persons"):

All G < F.
(All) D < F.

(All) D < G.

Since the trouble here lies with the minor premise, let us say this syllogism commits Fault 3: *misplaced inclusion*. It is like saying that the kitchen is in the house, and the grand piano is in the house; therefore, the grand piano must be in the kitchen. Just because two classes are both included in a third one, it doesn't follow that either of them is included in the other. That is the principle of guilt by association: the Weather underground was opposed to continued financing of war in Southeast Asia, and so were officers of SANE, so obviously the officers of SANE belonged (secretly) to the Weather underground.

Finally, someone might reason that

> Those who flee the scene of the crime are guilty persons, but the defendant did not flee; therefore, he is not guilty.

Or, in abbreviated form:

All F < G.
(All) D ≮ F.
―――――――
(All) D ≮ G.

In an A-major syllogism, no conclusion can be drawn if the minor premise places the third class outside the inner circle. This is Fault 4: *misplaced exclusion*. It is like saying that the kitchen is in the house, and the grand piano is not in the kitchen; therefore, the grand piano is not in the house. Just because a class is excluded from another class, it is not necessarily excluded from a class that includes the other class.

To master the art of syllogistic reasoning is not to master the art of reasoning. But it is a start. In fact, if you know how to think about classes and their relationships, you are well on your way to being a good thinker.

EXERCISE 9B

Which of the four faults—double particular (DP), double exclusion (DE), misplaced inclusion (MI), misplaced exclusion (ME)—is committed by the following syllogisms?

1. Undependable people are often likable, and so are some taxi drivers. Therefore, some taxi drivers are undependable.

2. Undependable people are often likable; and likable people are often generous; therefore, undependable people are often generous.

3. Not everyone who went to the party got smashed; none of those who got smashed went to work the next day; therefore, some of those who went to the party also went to work the next day.

4. All of the municipal judges over eighty years old have been retired; none of the fully competent municipal judges are over eighty years old; therefore, no fully competent municipal judge has been retired.

5. No philosophical materialist believes in freedom of the will; Hornsby is not a philosophical materialist; therefore, he believes in freedom of the will.

6. All of the new buildings in our city are more or less hideous; but some of the apartment houses are not new; therefore, they are not hideous.

7. Our opponents concede that some of their candidates have accepted money from the milk producers. But we know that all candidates who have promised to help the milk producers have accepted their contributions. Hence, some of our opponents' candidates must have promised to help the milk producers.

8. Thoughtless remarks are aggravating, which shows that Jones's remarks are never aggravating, since they are never thoughtless.

9. Within the general class of paintings, there are some that are not very original, and there are some that are very great; from which we may conclude that some very great paintings are not very original.

10. That the president is not competent may be seen from the following considerations: any president who would balance his budget would clearly be competent, but this president did not balance his budget.

EXERCISE 9C

Here are two syllogisms, one of which builds on the other by taking its conclusion as a premise. Write a paragraph of ordinary prose, presenting this compound argument as it might appear in an editorial. Recast the propositions in any way that seems natural and persuasive to you, and fill in with other sentences that might beef up the argument in a helpful way—perhaps by giving further reasons for some of these propositions. Study the differences between the bare syllogisms presented here and the argument as you present it.

All { persons whose possession of a handgun would constitute a danger to society } < { persons who should not be permitted to carry handguns } .

All { persons who go hunting for sport } ⊄ { persons whose possession of handguns would constitute a danger to society } .

All { persons who go hunting for sport } ⊄ { persons who should not be permitted to carry handguns } .

Some { persons who go hunting for sport } < { persons who have been convicted of violent crimes } .

Some { persons who have been convicted of violent crimes } ⊄ { persons who should not be permitted to carry handguns } .

EXERCISE 9D

What premises are omitted from the following syllogistic arguments?
State the premises explicitly.

1. Parents who help their children with their homework are laying the foundations for juvenile delinquency, for it inevitably weakens one's sense of responsibility to be excused from doing one's duty.

2. Unfortunately, my opponent's argument has a hidden premise that he has not stated explicitly; therefore, the conclusion is not acceptable.

3. Some of the accused members of the state highway commission must have been guilty of taking bribes. Otherwise, why would they have resigned when the investigation was started?

4. There is no need for the country to follow the sheepskin parade and send so many young people to college; we got along well enough a hundred years ago, when only a small percentage of people had college degrees.

5. Since to encourage the exploitation of natural resources is of benefit to the public, natural-gas producers should be freed from federal control.

10

SOME IFFY ARGUMENTS

conditional reasoning

What makes the word "if" such an important one in our thinking is just this: you often know that a conditional proposition is true without knowing (or before knowing) whether either of its two ingredient propositions is true. The ingredients of a conditional are (1) the proposition that follows the "if" (this is the *antecedent* of the conditional) and (2) the proposition that follows the "then" (the *consequent* of the conditional). In

If Susan drops the vase, (*then*) it will break,

"Susan drops (will drop) the vase" is the antecedent, and "(The vase) will break" is the consequent. You may not know whether Susan will drop the vase, but you do know that, being so fragile, it will not survive the impact on the kitchen floor. You may know (because you have been given adequate assurance) that

> *If* members of Friends of the Earth contribute generously to that
> organization, *then* it will lobby with Congress for effective control
> over strip mining.

Yet you may not know (as yet, anyway) whether the contributions will
be made or whether the lobbying will occur.

Now suppose you have a conditional proposition on hand that
could be used as one premise of a deductive argument; what will you do
with it? What other propositions could be combined with it in order to
obtain a valid conclusion? One possibility is to bring in other conditional
propositions that can be linked with it in a chain. For example:

> *If* members of FOE contribute generously, *then* FOE will lobby with ✓
> Congress for a bill to control strip mining.
> *If* FOE lobbies with Congress for a bill to control strip mining, *then*
> Congress will pass a bill to control strip mining.
> *If* Congress passes a bill to control strip mining, *then* hundreds of
> square miles of land will be preserved from destruction.
> _____
> *If* members of FOE contribute generously, *then* hundreds of square
> miles of land will be preserved from destruction.

The pattern is plain:

> If *P* then *Q*.
> If *Q* then *R*.
> If *R* then *S*.
> _____
> If *P* then *S*.

And its validity is also plain.

Arguments of this form are *conditional chains*. As usual, the chain
is no stronger than its weakest link. If any one of the premises is false or
shaky, the conclusion has not been established, even though the argument
is valid.

Though conditional chains can take us far in reasoning, they do not
liberate us from the realm of ifs. So long as we cannot justifiably affirm *P*,
we cannot affirm any of the other simple propositions by itself; we can
only say *if* such and such were true, *then* something else would be true.
But this suggests a rather different way in which we could obtain a conclusion with the help of our original conditional premise:

> *If* members of FOE contribute generously, *then* FOE will lobby with ✓
> Congress for a bill to control strip mining.
> Members of FOE will contribute generously.
> _____
> FOE will lobby with Congress for a bill to control strip mining.

Now we have a more definite conclusion: we actually make the prediction that the lobbying will occur. To obtain this conclusion, we needed two bits of information, which we might have acquired at different times and from different sources; we put them together and drew what is obviously a valid conclusion.

The form of this *conditional argument* is simple enough: in the minor premise we affirm the antecedent of the major premise, and we are then permitted, by way of conclusion, to affirm the consequent of the major premise.

> If *P* then *Q*.
> *P*.
> _____
> *Q*.

You may not have realized it, but this pattern of thinking is essential to many of your most familiar actions. When you push the elevator button to summon the elevator, you assume this premise: "If I push the elevator button, the elevator will come." And you try to make the consequent true by making the antecedent true.

But it doesn't work the other way around:

> If *P* then *Q*.
> *Q*.
> _____
> *P*.

For it may be true that if *P* then *Q*, and it may be true that *Q*—yet it may not be true that *P*. For example:

> If Susan drops the glass, then it will break.
> It just broke.
> _____
> Susan dropped it.

Wrong—actually, Henry is the one who (accidentally) broke the vase. The fault here is that of *affirming the consequent* in the minor premise: the conclusion does not follow.

You might think that affirming the consequent is sometimes all right. For example:

> If Congress passes this bill, then the president will veto it.
> The president will veto the bill.
> _____
> Congress will pass the bill.

This seems to make sense; but why? The argument, as it stands, is not really valid, but we tacitly make a common-sense assumption that *would* make a decent argument—namely, that the president can't veto a bill that has not been passed. When we make this our conditional premise, we are in good shape:

> If the president vetoes this bill, then Congress will pass (that is, will
>   already have passed) it.   ✓
> The president will veto the bill.
> _____
> Congress will pass the bill.

Do not confuse this argument with the previous one. The point is that when we wish to draw a deductive inference, we must be sure we have in our premises all that it takes to derive the hoped-for conclusion.

There remain two other forms of conditional argument to be considered. If you affirm the antecedent (minor premise), you can affirm the consequent (conclusion): this we have seen. If you *deny* the *consequent* (minor premise), you can deny the antecedent (conclusion):

> If *P* then *Q*.
> Not-*Q*.
> _____
> Not-*P*.

The major premise says that *P* can't be true without *Q* being true, so if it turns out that *Q* is not true, then *P* is not true. The inference is simple, yet it is the heart of some of our most vital reasoning—the kind of reasoning we do when we correct our own ideas, rejecting or revising them, because we discover that they have consequences that we cannot reasonably accept.

Suppose someone buys an expensive painting presumably by a Canadian painter named Furlong. He believes it is genuine (*P*). One day, an art expert tells him that if Furlong painted it, a small maple leaf with an "F" inside it will be found on the other side of the canvas in the lower left-hand corner (if *P* then *Q*). But no such mark is there (not-*Q*). The original belief has to be given up (not-*P*). Or suppose someone is convinced that human nature is inherently and irredeemably evil (*P*). As he thinks through the implications of his view, he comes to realize that if *P* is true, then there would be no such thing as conscience: no one would act out of a sense of moral obligation (if *P* then not-*Q*). But some persons do act in such a way (*Q*). Here, the consequent is a negative proposition, so its denial is affirmative. But the principle is the same.

This is in fact one of the most important ways of discovering or proving that a proposition is false: we show that if it were true, its consequence would conflict with some other proposition that is already known to be true. Of course, we must be quite sure that the supposed consequence really is a consequence—that the conditional premise really is true. When Patty Hearst was kidnapped by the Symbionese Liberation Army, it was widely suspected that Miss Hearst was a willing participant. In their book on the Hearst case (*Tania: The Revolution of Patty Hearst;* New York: Macmillan, 1974), Marilyn Baker and Sally Brompton remark:

> I didn't believe she was in on it. . . . Wouldn't a woman planning her own abduction wear more than just underpants and a bathrobe?

If you look closely, you can find two distinct arguments compressed into this remark. There is a syllogism that moves from a major premise about all women to a conclusion about Patty Hearst. And there is the conditional argument that denies the consequent:

> If Patty Hearst planned her own abduction, she was wearing more than underpants and a bathrobe.
> She was not wearing more than underpants and a bathrobe.
> _____
> Patty Hearst did not plan her own abduction.

This is valid, of course. Whether the conclusion is sound depends on the reliability of its conditional premise and on the generalization about women on which that premise ultimately rests.

Denying the consequent gets results, then; but what about *denying the antecedent?* This is another fault. The reason is plain: even though P is false, it doesn't follow that Q is false. Take a simple example:

> If Cornbread is in the vicinity of the bank tonight, then graffiti will appear on the side of the bank.
> Cornbread will not be in the vicinity of the bank tonight.
> _____
> Graffiti will not appear on the side of the bank.

But that's obviously too much to conclude: there is always the possibility that Kool Aid or Venango Kid will be around to write his own graffiti.

EXERCISE 10A

Which of the following conditional arguments are valid (V), and which are invalid, because they involve affirming the consequent (AC) or denying the antecedent (DA)?

1. If most doctors are opposed to Medicare, then it must be a bad policy. Most doctors apparently *are* opposed. Therefore, it is a bad policy.

2. Granted that if most of the people growing up in our big cities acquire a sense of purpose and meaningfulness, then ours is a healthy society. But it is not true that most of them acquire this sense, and that's why I say that our society is not healthy.

3. If capitalism is the best productive economic system, then West Germany may be expected to be very prosperous. West Germany *is* indeed very prosperous, which proves that capitalism is the most productive economic system.

4. If communism is the best form of government for human beings, then civil liberties are not important to human beings. But civil liberties *are* important; therefore, communism is not the best form of government.

5. If the Piltdown man is genuine, the bones have not been treated with potassium bichromate and iron salt, which they have; consequently, the Piltdown man is a fraud.

6. The refugee situation will be relieved, provided that the Immigration Act is repealed, but it won't be; it follows that the situation will not be relieved.

7. In the event that the government helps farms in the drought area, beef prices will be kept down. The government will help, and therefore prices will be kept down.

8. If the president's nominee for the position of federal judge is a man who defied the federal courts when he was governor (and he did), then his nomination should be rejected by the Senate Judiciary Committee.

9. Given that Jones is handsome and wealthy, he will make an ideal husband for Susan. He will in fact make an ideal husband for her—from which we may conclude that he is handsome and wealthy.

10. Without making a strong appeal for austerity, the president will not be able to persuade people to conserve scarce energy. But he has decided to make such an appeal; so people will conserve scarce energy.

A very powerful form of deductive reasoning is that which is commonly referred to as a "process of elimination." We already know that there are just three ways in which the burglar could have entered the apartment (through the door, the window, or the skylight); our investigation shows that he did not enter through the door, which was locked and bolted, or through the window, which was shut and latched; we conclude that he must have entered through the skylight. By eliminating all but one of the available alternatives, we leave the last one as the only possible (and therefore the necessary) conclusion.

Of course, an argument of this sort works only if (1) we really have listed all the available alternatives and (2) we really have eliminated all but one. A mistake about either of these assumptions will knock the ground (that is, a premise) out from under the argument.

We have here the basic pattern of inferences involving the word "or"—that is, the basic pattern of *alternative arguments*. In their simplest form, such arguments have a major premise presenting two alternatives, of which one is then eliminated by the minor premise, leaving the other to stand as a conclusion. The alternatives are stated as propositions. For example:

Either the military budget will be increased by several billion dollars *or* the new improved multiple-warhead missiles will be postponed. The military budget will *not* be increased by several billion dollars.

The new improved multiple-warhead missiles will be postponed.

As long as we make no further assumptions about the case, this process of elimination is the only valid way of drawing a conclusion. The major premise tells us that at least one of its two propositions is true; it tells us no more. Thus we cannot reason this way:

Either the military budget will be increased by several billion dollars *or* the new improved multiple-warhead missiles will be postponed. The military budget *will* be increased by several billion dollars.

The new improved multiple-warhead missiles will *not* be postponed.

Here the minor premise *affirms*, rather than denies, one of the propositions in the major premise, and the conclusion *denies*, rather than affirms, the other. But nothing in the premises warrants this conclusion. They do not give us complete information about the Pentagon's planning; even if the military budget is increased, other considerations may lead to a postponement of the development of the new missiles.

In short, in an alternative argument, a conclusion may be drawn by denying one of the propositions in the major premise, but not by affirming one. The logical fault may be called *affirming an alternative.*

Yet there is a complication, and if you are to be master of the word "or" rather than its unwitting victim, you must keep this complication in mind. Consider the burglar argument again.

> *Either* the burglar entered through the door *or* he entered through the window *or* he entered through the skylight. ✓
> The burglar did *not* enter through the door and he did *not* enter through the window.
> ___
> He entered through the skylight.

That's fine. But now imagine a somewhat different situation. Keep the same major premise: we know there were only three possible ways in. But suppose we examine the window and find that it has been jimmied open since we left the apartment, and indeed is wide open, with a fire escape just outside it. We have good evidence, in short, that the burglar entered by the window. We then reason as follows:

> *Either* the burglar entered through the door *or* he entered through the window *or* he entered through the skylight.
> The burglar entered through the window.
> ___
> He did *not* enter through the door and he did *not* enter through the skylight.

On the face of it, this argument commits the fault of affirming an alternative. Yet it is quite convincing. Why so?

Clearly, we are making another assumption here, relying on a hidden premise that hasn't been explicitly stated: namely, that the burglar entered only once, and consequently by only one route. Of course this is not self-evident; it is just very likely. We can imagine a most incompetent and forgetful burglar who breaks into the apartment by jimmying the window, departs by way of the fire escape with the portable TV set, but leaves his burglar kit behind. Later, he remembers this lapse, but forgets that he went in through the window the first time (or perhaps finds the fire escape occupied by an off-duty policeman he knows); so he breaks in through the door to recover his professional equipment. Perhaps this story seems far-fetched; even so, it reveals the additional premise we are taking for granted: that only one of the three alternative propositions listed in the major premise is true. The alternatives, in other words, are assumed to be *exclusive.*

Now we can set forth the whole argument, assumption and all—but for simplicity, let us limit the alternatives to two:

It is not the case that the burglar entered both through the door and through the window. ✓
[That is, *either* the burglar did not enter through the door *or* he did not enter through the window.]
The burglar entered through the window.

The burglar did *not* enter through the door.

This argument is perfectly valid. It does not affirm an alternative, as the alternatives now appear, but denies one.

The lesson is this: when the context of an alternative argument makes it clear that the two alternatives are exclusive of each other (that not more than one of them is true), we can derive a valid conclusion, because we can use as a premise the proposition that at least one of the alternatives is false. But without such assurance we cannot.

There is a form of argument that combines alternative and conditional elements in a useful way, and we should take a brief look at it. In this form of argument, two or more alternatives are presented, and then certain consequences of each are also presented. For example:

Either the Federal Reserve Board will lower interest rates or it will raise interest rates ✓
If it raises interest rates, inflation will increase.
If it lowers interest rates, unemployment will increase.

Either inflation will increase or unemployment will increase.

Never mind the technicalities of this economic argument: the premises may be false or oversimplified, but we are concerned with validity. This form of argument is the *dilemma:* it puts you in a bind, because you have to choose between two alternatives, generally unpleasant ones. (Of course, you could look on the bright side and say that raising the rates will decrease unemployment, and lowering rates will decrease inflation.)

Sometimes, a dilemma presents a Hobson's choice—that is, a choice between alternatives that both lead (it is claimed) to the same unfortunate result:

Either inflation will increase or unemployment will increase. ✓
If inflation increases, voters will be unhappy.
If unemployment increases, voters will be unhappy.

Voters will be unhappy [either way].

EXERCISE 10B

In some of the following arguments, the conclusion is validly drawn because the minor premise denies an alternative (D). Others may be considered valid because the alternatives presented in the major premise may be assumed to be exclusive (E). Still others are invalid (I). Which are which?

1. Stanley was born in either North Dakota or South Dakota. He was born in North Dakota. Therefore, he was not born in South Dakota.

2. Tomorrow's weather: either some rain or some snow. Later prediction: rain tomorrow. So, no snow.

3. His latest work is either a novel or a chemistry textbook. You say it's not a novel? Then it must be a chemistry textbook.

4. Jones either married into wealth or inherited a lot of money. He did marry into wealth, I learn. Thus, he did not inherit a lot of money.

5. The witness either lied to the grand jury or he had an honest lapse of memory. He did not lie. He must have had a lapse of memory.

6. Copernicus was born in either the fifteenth or the sixteenth century. You say he was born in the fifteenth century? Then he couldn't have been born in the sixteenth century.

7. Under the new election-finance laws, the incumbent senator will either have to draw heavily on his own savings or else rely largely on small contributions. Evidently the latter will be the case, for he refuses to use his own savings.

8. It's impossible for you to act fairly and at the same time please everybody in this difficult case. Luckily, since you have resolved not to try to please everybody, your action is bound to be at least fair.

9. The alternatives that face us are (1) to accept the court's verdict and pay the fine imposed or (2) to appeal the decision to a higher court. Given the strength of our case, we have decided to do the latter; therefore, we shall not be doing the former.

10. On the one hand, we might cope with the energy crisis by urging people to cut down on consumption of gasoline. On the other hand, we could search for forms of energy other than fossil fuel. We shall certainly do the latter; it follows that we shall not be doing the former.

EXERCISE 10C

Write a short essay embodying a dilemma. In one paragraph, argue that only two alternatives are possible (say, that the school board must either refuse to increase teachers' salaries or else cut back on various special educational programs). In succeeding paragraphs, argue that certain consequences will follow from each of these alternatives. Then draw the conclusion.

EXERCISE 10D

Write a short essay developing a conditional chain argument. Carry it through at least five steps, and try to make it as convincing as possible, by giving reasons to support each conditional premise—that is, to show that the consequent really will follow if the antecedent occurs. Your essay might deal, for example, with the long-range consequences of an ecological misstep (say, widespread use of certain pesticides or of aerosol sprays), or of a form of miseducation, or of an objectionable government policy.

11

GOING OUT ON A LIMB

generalization

A form of inference that turns up frequently can be illustrated by the following examples:

You *see* the scales being scraped from a salmon at a fish market. You *infer* that all salmon have scales.

You *read* five detective stories by Ross Macdonald, and judge them exciting. You *infer* that all his detective stories are exciting.

You *notice*, while driving along the Pennsylvania Turnpike at fifty-five miles an hour (the legal limit), that half the cars you see are passing you. You *infer* that half of all drivers on that turnpike exceed the speed limit.

You *are told* that a spot check of eighty Baltimore welfare recipients turned up ten who were earning more money than they are allowed to, in view of the payments they receive. You *infer* that one eighth of all welfare recipients in the city are doing the same.

When you make inferences like these, you are *generalizing*. The basis of the inference is (or is assumed to be) a fact about a single object or event, or about a class of objects or events. The inference reaches out to encompass a larger class.

Never mind for the moment whether these inferences are warranted. Before coming to that question, we must be as clear as possible about what is going on here, logically speaking. Three things are involved in all generalizing: two classes, one of which is included in the other, and one property that the generalizer is interested in.

Generalizing has a direction; it proceeds from one class (even if that class has but one member) to a second, more inclusive class. The larger class, which is what the generalization is about, is called the *target population*. A population doesn't have to consist of people: it can be fish or detective stories, as well as car drivers or welfare recipients. When you generalize, it is essential that you have clearly in mind exactly what target population you are generalizing about. In the examples above, they are:

$\left\{\begin{array}{l}\text{salmon}\\ \text{detective stories by Ross Macdonald}\\ \text{drivers on the Pennsylvania Turnpike}\\ \text{welfare recipients in Baltimore}\end{array}\right\}$

The result of generalizing is a conclusion about the nature of the target population—more specifically, that a certain property is distributed in a certain way throughout that target population. This *projected property* may be:

the property of having scales
the property of being exciting (to read)
the property of exceeding the turnpike speed limit
the property of earning more than the welfare rules allow

The generalizer may conclude that *every* member of the target population has this projected property—in which case his conclusion is a universal proposition:

All salmon have scales.
All detective novels by Ross Macdonald are exciting.

Or the generalizer may conclude that some *portion* of the target population has this projected property—in which case the conclusion is a *statistical* proposition:

Fifty percent of all drivers on the Pennsylvania Turnpike exceed the legal fifty-five-mile-an-hour speed limit.

One eighth of Baltimore welfare recipients earn more than the welfare rules allow.

The class *from* which the generalization is launched, so to speak, consists of those members of the target population that you already know something about: they constitute a *sample* of the target population:

one scaly salmon
five exciting detective stories by Ross Macdonald
a number of persons driving on the Pennsylvania Turnpike
eighty Baltimore welfare recipients

A *generalization*, then, is a proposition about the distribution of some projected property in a target population, a proposition reached by inference from information about the distribution of that property in a sample of the population. And a generalization is warranted—is logically justified—when the sample is a *representative* sample of the population; that is, when it reflects the composition of the whole. An ideal generalization might be pictured in this way:

POPULATION

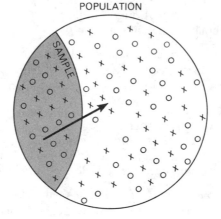

The arrow shows the direction of inference, from the sample to the rest of the population. The members of the population consist of circles and crosses. If we were to let the circles stand for turnpike drivers who obey the speed limit, and the crosses for those who exceed it, then the sample would be a perfectly representative one: for half the marks in it are crosses, and half the marks in the whole population are crosses, too.

Those particular things that are known to have the projected property are *instances* of the generalization:

This scaly salmon is an instance of the generalization, "All salmon have scales."

This driver now going over fifty-five miles an hour on the Pennsylvania Turnpike is an instance of the generalization, "Fifty percent of all drivers on the Pennsylvania Turnpike exceed the legal fifty-five-mile-an-hour speed limit."

Of course, a single thing can be an instance of many possible generalizations. For example:

This driver now going over fifty-five miles an hour on the Pennsylvania Turnpike is an instance of the generalization, "All drivers on the Pennsylvania Turnpike exceed the legal fifty-five-mile-an-hour speed limit."

You can see why generalizing is difficult. Given the instances we have, which generalization shall we fit them to? Of course, when we find a driver going *under* the speed limit, he cannot be an instance of the universal generalization above. In fact, he is a *counter-instance* to it: he is an exception to that generalization, for if there is at least one law-abiding driver, then not all drivers can be violating the speed law. Usually, when we generalize we will find some things that are instances of our generalization and some that are not, and our problem is to decide which generalization to believe in the light of that mixed evidence.

EXERCISE 11A

What are the target population, the sample, and the projected property in each of the following generalizations?

1. As the cans of Vichyssoise soup come off the production line at the soup factory, the inspector picks out one every fifteen or twenty minutes (one in every thousand or twelve hundred cans), opens it, tests it, and finds it free of harmful bacteria. He passes them all as safe.

2. After examining a selection of fifty episodes from television comedy series, and noting that in forty-five of them there are explicit or implicit assumptions of male superiority to women with respect to intelligence and good sense, the psychologist concludes that ninety percent of television dramatic fare is sexist.

3. The sociologist studying police-community relations spends ten weekend nights riding in a police car and observing the way the police respond to calls. Out of a hundred and forty-three incidents in which the police are called upon to take physical action (stopping a fight, arresting a suspected burglar, and so forth), he observes only six in which the degree of force used could be questioned as possibly excessive. This shows, according to his report, that in about ninety-six percent of their actions police act within the law.

4. The economist examines the list of wholesale fruit and vegetable distributors in the yellow pages of a big-city telephone directory. Of 109 companies listed under personal names, 29 have Italian names. This convinces him that approximately a quarter of such distributors in all cities are owned or operated by Italians.

5. After dropping into his neighborhood bar and asking six customers what they think of the present administration in Washington, the newspaper reporter decides that the general public is opposed to the administration's policies by a ratio of two to one.

How do you generalize successfully? In other words, how do you manage to achieve generalizations that will continue to be dependable as times goes by—that will not run afoul of new experiences and observations? There are no rules to guarantee the success of generalizing. But there are well-known pitfalls to avoid. And if you make a serious and persistent effort to avoid those pitfalls, you stand a good chance, on the whole, of making generalizations that are soundly based and likely to stand the test of time.

Suppose you are curious to know what percentage (roughly) of the students in your local community college have smoked pot. It would take too much time and trouble to ask all four thousand or so of them. So to obtain any generalization about the entire population, you'll need a sample. The question is, how to choose that sample?

But even before this question arises, you will have to consider how you can obtain relevant instances of a generalization. For example, the best procedure would seem to be to ask some of the students about their experience. But right at that point there may be trouble. Some of those who have smoked pot won't admit it, because they are afraid of what their parents would say or of possible legal penalties. Others will claim that they have smoked pot, even though they haven't, because they want to be with it and because they feel embarrassed not to have kept up with their more daring peers. Perhaps these obstacles can be largely overcome, or at least diminished, if you can convince the students that you have a serious purpose and that the truth would be worth having (say, in developing an argument for more humane laws regarding marijuana), and if you can assure them that their replies will be absolutely confidential (say, by handing them questionnaires to fill out anonymously and deposit in a mailbox when no one is around). Many a questionnaire, even some prepared by social scientists, has foundered because such precautions were not adequately taken.

In the end, you will have to make a judgment about the reliability of your sample: that is, how closely the answers you obtain correspond to actuality. And any error at this stage may be magnified when you generalize. So if you have reason to believe that many of the students are lying to you, you may have to abandon the project—or at least note very clearly that your conclusion is subject to a considerable margin of error.

But let's suppose you obtain the statements, and accept them (tentatively) as true. Then you will have a number of cases of students who have smoked pot, and a number of cases of students who have not smoked pot. These constitute your sample.

But, of course, not any old sample will serve. What can you do to obtain the best possible sample—the sample most likely to be representative of the whole student body? There are three principles to follow.

1. Scatter your sample. Select your sample by chance: that is what is meant by scattering. Before you deal the cards, you shuffle them so that the hands will not be hand-picked; rather, they will be the result of accident. The cannery inspector selects his sample cans at random; thus, he has no reason to think that they are any different, as a group, from the rest of the cans. The same principle applies to your investigation: you don't want to select only students who are especially eager to be interviewed, or who are especially shy about being interviewed, or who hang around the Hofbrau after school, or who are prominent in sports. You need a method of selection that will give you students of all sorts and conditions. So you might stop them at random in the hallway and ask if they will cooperate. Or you might select every tenth name from the college directory, write them on slips of paper, put them in a hat, stir them up, and have your three-year-old niece pick them out one at a time until you have enough. This way, everyone in the college stands a theoretically equal chance of being included; the sample is just about as unbiased as it can be.

The following diagram represents a population in which the crosses (pot smokers) are unevenly distributed. Note how the scattered sample, selected randomly, presents a fairly good picture of the whole.

POPULATION

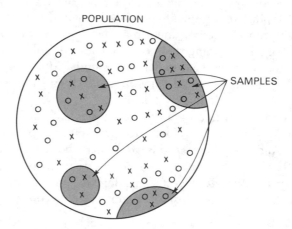

SAMPLES

2. *Spread your sample.* If your target population is very homo-geneous—practically all white upper-middle-class suburban teen-agers—your task is somewhat simplified: what you find to be true of any random sample of it is fairly likely to be true of the whole. Yet even in that case, some of the population will be male and some female; and there will be differences in economic status, educational level of parents, satis-factoriness of home life, and so on. Every population has its subclasses; the members differ from one another in various ways. The question is, which of these differences *might make a difference* in pot-smoking behavior? Maybe sex is a significant factor: it may be that girls are brought up to be less competitive than boys. Wealth may be a sig-nificant factor, since not all students can afford to buy pot. Religious training, racial ancestry, ethnic group—these and other factors may be highly relevant. If you pick your sample from the wealthiest students with divorced parents, you will probably obtain a biased result; if you pick your sample from poor female students with a deeply religious background, your sample may well be biased another way.

How do you guard against these biases? Of course, you can't take into account all possible differences that might be significant, but you must take into account the main ones that you can think of. Make sure, then, that your sample includes representative members of all those subclasses: rich and poor, Christian and non-Christian, white and black, male and female, from broken homes and from unbroken homes, and so on. That is what I mean by *spreading* the sample. Think of it in the following way: if pot smoking is distributed as unevenly as the crosses in the following diagram, then only a spread-out sample such as is pictured would capture that distribution. By cutting across the four strata separated by horizontal lines, the sample reflects the uneven distribution in the target population.

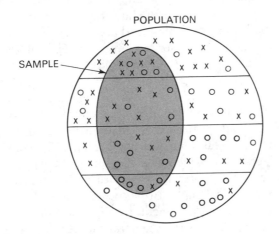

And when you encounter someone else's generalization, always look carefully at the sample on which it is based, and ask yourself whether you know any reason why the sample may not be typical of the target population. So the strawberries on top of the basket are large and luscious-looking? But we don't infer that the ones underneath must be just like them—for we know that storekeepers tend to put the best ones on top.

Sometimes, the first and second principles have to be adjusted to each other. For example, you might first take a random sample, then go over it to make sure that it contains at least some representatives of major subclasses, and keep making it larger until it does. Or you might first mark out the major subclasses and take a random sample from each.

3. *Stretch your sample.* Even spreading and scattering will not be enough unless your sample is large enough to include representatives of the various subclasses of the population. The sample must be of substantial size, relative to the size of the population. Two very general principles apply here: (1) the larger and more varied the population, the larger the sample should be; (2) the larger the sample from any given population, the more likely the conclusion is to be true. No more can be said in general without getting into mathematics. Obviously, a sample of one won't do: anyone who generalizes about a population from a single instance is asking for error:

Last night I saw Peter Bogdanovich's latest film, and thought it stupid and pretentious. Obviously, he has no talent as a film maker.

The sample consists of one film; the conclusion is a proposition, apparently, about all films so far made and yet to be made by this director. But we are given no information to show that this film is typical of his work. It might be his one bad film; perhaps he had financial difficulties, or lost one of his leading actresses in mid-flight. The inference is a clear case of the fault known as *hasty generalization*.

When you write a composition that aims to support one or more generalizations, you will presumably be trying to make your argument convincing. The more careful you are to make clear exactly what you are generalizing about, and what you are generalizing from, the better your reader can follow your reasoning and see its merit. The convincingness of the argument depends on a judicious adjustment between the claim and the evidence that supports it. And where there is a danger (as in hasty generalization) of a logical gap between generalization and data, the gap can be narrowed—and the argument strengthened—in two ways. First, if you are bent on proving a strong generalization, say that

No (or hardly any) famous figures in American history have been admirable people,

then you must insure that the sample from which you generalize is sufficiently sizable, widely spread, and scattered to warrant your conclusion. Second, if you find that you can't come up with good enough evidence for *that* generalization, you can always scale it down and substitute a more cautious one:

Most famous figures in American history were not very admirable.

When, as often happens, the generalization is a topic sentence, you may be tempted to make it strong and striking; but don't do so unless you have the facts to back it up.

EXERCISE 11B

Here are some generalizations and the samples on which they are based. In each case, give a reason why the sample may not be typical of the target population.

1. *Generalization:* The selections performed by this rock group tonight are lacking in zest, drive, and tension.
   Sample: The first three pieces performed by this group tonight.

2. *Generalization:* Nearly every street in Old Haven has large potholes in it.
   Sample: Thirty blocks observed while driving through Old Haven.

3. *Generalization:* The behavior of this student is generally awkward and nervous.
   Sample: Behavior observed during an interview for a fellowship to study abroad.

4. *Generalization:* A large percentage of fire-department calls are false alarms.
   Sample: Calls turned in on three successive Saturday nights in August.

5. *Generalization:* Seventy-two percent of the women in Portbridge believe that abortion is morally justifiable.
   Sample: Fifty women encountered randomly in a local shopping center and asked, "Are there circumstances under which you would say a woman has the right to have an abortion?"

EXERCISE 11C

Plan and conduct a poll among the members of some group to which you belong; try to discover, say, the prevailing opinion on some current issue. Write up your results in the form of a report, explaining how you chose your sample in accordance with the three principles formulated in this chapter, and defending the reliability of your results.

12

THE REASON WHY

explanation

When the baggage finally makes its appearance at the end of an airplane trip, the suitcases tend to disappear rapidly as their owners hasten to reclaim them. But imagine one large suitcase sitting there for hours; no one comes to take it away. At the end of the day, an attendant will have to open it (it isn't locked) and try to identify the owner. Suppose that's your job: you open it and find inside nothing but fourteen liverwurst sandwiches and a blowtorch. You would undoubtedly be somewhat puzzled. How did these oddly associated items come to be there?

To be puzzled is to be in want of an explanation. The word "explanation" has a very broad meaning and covers a variety of activities: we explain the meaning of a poem, the process of refining oil into gasoline, the rules of canasta. But here we are concerned with explanation in a narrower sense—the sense in which we explain why something happened (an event) or why something is the way it is (a state of affairs).

Why is the television picture so distorted? Someone nearby is using a defective piece of electrical equipment.
How did the sidewalk come to be cracked? A heavy truck drove over it.
What accounts for the spots on Johnny's tongue? Johnny has measles.
Why did the president authorize the sale of atomic power plants to Egypt? He wanted the Sadat government to have a favorable attitude toward the United States.

You might not think very highly of these explanations. They are quite simple—perhaps too simple. But they serve as examples of the three essential ingredients of an explanation.

First, there must be something to be explained—something that has happened (such as spots appearing on the tongue), or something that is the case (such as the sidewalk's having a crack in it). This event or state of affairs is the *explainee*. And, obviously, explanation can't begin without one: you can't explain how the elephant got up the tree if there is no elephant in the tree.

Second, there must be something that does the explaining—an event (such as a heavy truck's driving over the sidewalk) or a state of affairs (such as certain bacteria being present in Johnny's body). This event or state is the *explainer*. When we are told of it, we understand how the explainee could have come about. Our puzzlement is assuaged.

But the explainee has to be clear and definite enough to serve its purpose. To give an explanation is to offer a proposition—that such and such explains so and so:

The presence of bacteria in Johnny's body *explains* Johnny's having spots on his tongue.

That's definite enough. But too often, people are content with so-called explanations that are far too vague and loose to explain anything:

Why did the Republicans lose so heavily in the last election? Because of voter apathy.
Why is crime rising? It's due to a general decline in morality.
Why does Henry bite his nails? He's a nervous type.

Expressions such as "voter apathy," "decline in morality," and "nervous type" might satisfy someone who is not very critical, but they are nearly empty phrases. How do we tell when morality has declined? What are the indications of decline? It's hard to pin down the explainer so that we can be sure that it really does explain what it is supposed to. Of course, when the question is very general, the answer is bound to be general, too. But we must be on guard against fake all-purpose "explainers" that merely stifle curiosity without satisfying it—for example, talk about fate, luck, bellicose instincts, "the establishment," and "the American way of life."

In the brief examples above, the explainee and the explainer are plainly presented, in that order, as question and as answer. The third ingredient of the explanation is unexpressed. Yet it is equally essential. To see what it is, we need only contrast the following "explanations":

> Why is the television picture so distorted? People are eating pizza in the next block.
> How did the sidewalk come to be cracked? Someone sneezed here yesterday.
> What accounts for the spots on Johnny's tongue? Last year was a bad year for the blueberry industry.
> Why did the president authorize the sale of atomic power plants to Egypt? He wanted to crack down on pornography.

What's wrong here? There doesn't seem to be any connection between the explainer and the explainee, so we don't feel that our question has really been answered. Question: How far is it to Kansas City? Answer: Peoria is twenty miles. But that's no answer to the question. What have pizzas to do with television pictures, or sneezes with sidewalk cracks? Is the blueberry industry relevant to tongue spots? How could anyone think that pornography would be discouraged by selling atomic power plants?

What is missing, then, is a proposition that will connect explainer with explainee—that will bridge the gap between them. And it must be a conditional proposition that will tell us that the explainee depends upon the explainer. Call it the *conditional bridge*.

> A heavy truck drove over the sidewalk. (*Explainer*)
> If a heavy truck drove over the sidewalk, then the sidewalk is cracked. (*Conditional bridge*)
> _____
> The sidewalk is cracked. (*Explainee*)

We have here our old acquaintance (from Chapter 10), the conditional argument. But this time we are not using it as a deductive argument to prove its conclusion. We don't need to prove that the sidewalk is cracked; we can see that. In fact, that's what started us wondering in the first place. What we *are* proving, or at least showing, is that *if* our explainer happened, *then* our explainee had to come about.

The same is true of our other examples. In explaining Johnny's spots by ascribing them to measles, we are assuming that:

If Johnny has measles, then he has spots on his tongue.

In the other examples, we are assuming that:

If someone nearby is using a defective piece of electrical equipment, then the television picture is distorted.

If the president wanted the Sadat government to have a favorable attitude toward the United States, then he authorized the sale of atomic power plants to Egypt.

You might think that these conditional propositions ought to proceed the other way: if Johnny has spots, then he has measles. Not so. The reason for this will be clearer as we proceed, but the main point is just that when we undertake to account for an event or state of affairs, we must show that it *had to follow* from whatever event or condition we offer as an explainer. We are not claiming that the explanation we give is the *only* explanation that could be given (there are other ways of cracking a sidewalk). We *are* claiming that the explanation we give is an adequate one, that it would in fact explain what it is supposed to explain; thus, it enables us to understand why the explainee occurred.

An explanation, evidently, is no better than its conditional bridge. Unless we have good reason to think that the conditional bridge is true, we can't put much stock in our explanation. If our readers will challenge, or will not accept, our conditional bridge, they will reject the explanation. What sort of evidence do we need, then, to back up the conditional bridge? Here, we have to rely on what we already know (our previous generalizations) about the way things behave. We might need specialized knowledge, such as that of the doctor who diagnoses Johnny's illness. Or we might need common experience of, say, trucks and their usual effects. It's not true that every time a truck drives over a sidewalk, the sidewalk cracks. But suppose the sidewalk before us is a fairly old and poorly made sidewalk, and some of the gravel underneath has washed out. And let us picture a very heavy tractor-trailer truck trying to make a turn while avoiding a car parked too close to the corner. Under those circumstances, the chances of cracking are extremely good. Our conditional bridge is pretty reasonable. But it would not be reasonable to accept the following conditional bridge:

If someone sneezed here yesterday, the sidewalk is cracked.

When you offer an explanation, then, make clear what is your explainee and what is your explainer—and, above all, make sure you have some solid evidence to support the conditional bridge that connects the explainee with the explainer.

EXERCISE 12A

What is the explainee, the explainer, and the conditional bridge in the following explanations?

1. Why has Don been so irritable lately?
   Too much coffee, I guess.

2. Why was Mabel late for work today?
   Her alarm clock didn't go off at its usual time.

3. "Who killed cock robin? 'I,' said the sparrow, 'with my bow and arrow.'

4. Why did the traffic policeman put a ticket on this car? It was too near the fire hydrant, apparently.

5. This door is stuck again. It must be the hot and humid weather.

6. It seems the boss has fired Spilch, though I thought he was the favorite. Spilch's work had been going downhill.

7. The stain on the rug? Coffee.

8. This bridge must have been washed out by the flood last spring.

9. The Phillies' failure to win the pennant, despite their good pitching, is to be accounted for by the injuries of several key players.

10. To understand the bat's ability to fly in the dark, we must know that it sends out sound waves that bounce back and warn it of obstacles.

So far, we have seen what is involved in presenting an explanation; but of course when we are puzzled, we don't just want *an* explanation, we want *the* explanation—that is, the correct or true explanation. The distinction is one that it is not wise to neglect. If you grab the first explanation that comes along, without asking whether there are better ones, you may be badly fooled.

An event might be explained in several ways; that is, several different explainers might be possible. How did the fire start? Perhaps: (1) a short circuit overheating the electrical system, (2) a gas leak, (3) a carelessly tossed cigarette, (4) a spark from the fireplace, (5) the act of an arsonist, or even a professional "torch." Some explanations are better than others. And, presumably, one explanation is the right one, if we can only discover which it is.

Selecting the right explanation is a process of choosing among available alternatives; it involves a form of the alternative argument, which we looked into earlier. In the usual case, we try to think of *possible* explainers—at least, those that occur to us as candidates. We then consider whether we know anything that rules out some of them. For example, investigation might show that there was no fire in the fireplace at the time, so our fourth explanation won't do. We learn that the house had been checked for gas leaks only that morning, so it looks as though our second explanation has to be set aside. By a process of elimination, we hope to rule out every plausible explanation but one, and that remaining one will then become acceptable.

When we eliminate each possible explanation, we are using another of our valid conditional arguments: that in which we deny the consequent. We reason:

If the fire was started by sparks from the fireplace, then there was
   a fire in the fireplace.
But there was no fire in the fireplace.

The fire was not started by sparks from the fireplace.

And:

If the fire was started by a gas leak, then the house was not checked
   for gas leaks that morning.
But the house *was* checked for gas leaks that morning.

The fire was not started by a gas leak.

It is this form of reasoning that shows us how the explanation runs afoul of the facts. But to use it we must have (1) facts and (2) reliable conditional premises.

There is nothing mechanical or open-and-shut about this elimination process. We may not have thought of all the possible alternatives; so we haven't *proved* that the fire was due to a short in the electrical system, even if that is the only remaining theory on our list. We may have made a mistake in ruling out some of the alternatives: for instance, it's conceivable (though unlikely) that the gas leak developed after the gas was checked. Yet we have to start with something, try out the available alternatives, make the best judgments we can, and come up with an explanation that seems the most reasonable one—or, failing that, at least narrow down our list to two or three. Every step is an inference and involves some risk of error, so all our conclusions have a provisional air— they are to be accepted for the time being, until we learn more about the situation.

Suppose, then, that we are left with two or more possible explanations, and we want to know which of them is most likely to be true; or that we are left with one, but we are by no means sure that it is the only possibility, and yet we still would like to know how much confidence to place in it. What do we do next? We ask three questions.

1. How common is the explainer? I don't know whether more fires are started by short circuits or by gas leaks; but this must be a matter of record somewhere. So if we had no other information at all about our fire, beyond the fact that there was a fire, we could at least say that the gas-leak explanation is better than the short-circuit explanation *if* fires started by gas leaks are more common—statistically more frequent—than fires started by short circuits. Carelessly tossed cigarettes seem to start quite a few fires, surely more than deliberate arsonists (even professional ones) do; so the arson theory is placed low on our list, and becomes a kind of last resort if the more common ones fail us.

Some proposed explanations can (tentatively) be rejected out of hand, just because the explainer is so uncommon, and much more common explainers are readily available. The stain in the rug (apart from any other information we might have about it) can be explained by spilled coffee or catsup; so why bring in whale oil or a rare vintage of red burgundy—unless we have some other reason to think that these have been on the scene lately? The most common explainer may not be the true one, of course; but it is a good one to start with.

2. How simple is the explainer? The short-circuit theory of the fire includes some assumptions about the presence of an electrical circuit and some overload of current. The arson theory includes a plot of some sort, various intentions of (perhaps) various persons, and so forth. One of these explainers is a good deal simpler than the other, in that it involves fewer persons, actions, events, and objects. Comparative simplicity is not always easy to estimate, especially if the explanations are very different. But sometimes we can make this judgment. And the logical principle to follow is this: do not accept the more complicated explanation if a simpler one is available to do the same job.

They must do the same job. If the fire-insurance company investigators discover some kerosene cans that apparently were not in the house yesterday, the arson theory will account for their presence but the short-circuit theory will not. So the short-circuit theory may be too simple—unless the cans can be explained in some other way. In any case, it is generally good to start with a simple explanation and to carry it as far as it can go. If the evidence runs against it, it will have to be abandoned in favor of a more complicated explanation. But that should be no *more* complicated than it has to be. Why jump to the conclusion that the fire was set by six arsonists, or by the CIA, or by a White House "plumbers" team—if one defective wire is enough to do the job?

3. *Does the explanation check out?* Sitting down and thinking of a lot of possible explanations for something—a fire, a headache, the tendency of a car to stall, a revolution abroad—is armchair theorizing. And a very important thing it is. But it's not enough, by itself, to get us to the truth. Even after we have weighed the various theories for their commonness and simplicity, we need to take a further step before accepting any one of them: we must check out the explanation.

If the explanation of the fire is the correct one, it makes a difference: it has consequences that we can test. If Jones poisoned his wife, he must have gotten the poison somewhere; so we might check recent purchases in nearby drugstores. If the car's battery is dead, then the horn won't make its usual sound when we try it out. If the moon is as old as the earth, then the thermoluminescence test will show the moon rocks to be at least three billion years old. And so on. With the help of conditionals such as these, we don't have to accept an explanation until we have tested it. It may seem perfectly plausible, and we may even want to believe it, but we need independent evidence before we decide that it is the *best* explanation—that is, the one most likely to be true.

When you write a composition in which you try to convince the reader of a certain explanation, you will probably do most of your thinking (along the lines sketched in this chapter) before you start to write—though when you start to lay out your argument, you may get some new ideas or see flaws in the ones you already have. Yet the thinking you have done will be reflected in your writing: if you don't have a very clear idea of just what you are trying to explain and of what your explanation is, if you haven't considered the commonness and simplicity of your explanation, if you are not sure how to check it out—then your composition is likely to be as muddled as your state of mind. The more you think things through, however, the better organized your composition will be, and the more likely your reader is to be enlightened and convinced.

About those liverwurst sandwiches and the blow torch: frankly, I haven't figured that out yet myself.

EXERCISE 12B

Here are some explainees, and a pair of explainers for each. Compare them with respect to commonness and simplicity. Suggest a way of checking out each.

1. *Explainee:* A sudden sharp, loud sound is heard in a street nearby.
   Explanation A: A car backfired.
   Explanation B: Someone fired a gun.

2. *Explainee:* The painting is in the style of Picasso's "blue period," was bought by the museum from a reputable dealer, and is signed "Picasso."
   Explanation A: Picasso painted it.
   Explanation B: A clever forger painted it.

3. *Explainee:* The governor has vetoed the liberalized abortion bill.
   Explanation A: He believes that fetuses have a right to life.
   Explanation B: He is catering to a vocal segment of public opinion in order to be reelected.

4. *Explainee:* John, an A student, and Joe, a C student, handed in very similar answers to the examination after sitting side by side while taking it.
   Explanaton A: Joe copied his answer from John.
   Explanation B: John tutored Joe the night before, and Joe happened to study especially carefully the subjects asked about on the examination.

5. *Explainee:* Jones is unusually irritable this morning.
   Explanation A: Jones did not get his customary amount of sleep last night.
   Explanation B: Jones read in this morning's paper that a distant uncle, whose money he had hoped to inherit, had just died and left his entire estate to his cook.

EXERCISE 12C

Read carefully the newspaper accounts of a recent inquiry into some puzzling occurrence—say, the collision of two ships, the crash of an airliner, the firing of a public official, a murder, the deplorable state of nursing homes. Write an essay analyzing the evidence for various alternative explanations that are under consideration, and judging the comparative strength of these hypotheses according to the three principles presented in this chapter.

13

HOW COME?

cause and effect

Quite often, when we are puzzled and seek understanding, we ask about the causes of things—of specific events (what caused the car to stall? the student to fail? the tree to die?) or of states of affairs (what caused the seas to be salt? the car to be dented? the teacher to have such a bad disposition?) More often than not, when we ask such questions, we are troubled by what we have found—the effect confronting us—and we seek the cause because we want to eliminate the effect (inflation), prevent similar things from happening in the future (pneumonia), or have a warning the next time around (earthquakes). But it is not only undesirable things whose causes we may wish to know; it is useful to understand how good things came about, too.

The questions I have cited as examples are of the same basic type: they are questions about the cause of a specific event or state. This is the sort of question we shall consider first, before going on to consider general causal questions, which concern not individual events or states but *kinds* of event or state.

What is a cause? Since a significant portion of our thinking, and hence our writing, has to do with causes (and their effects), it will pay us to try to be clear about what they are. I shall shortly note some serious logical confusions that we can easily fall into unless we take pains to understand the notion of cause.

The cause of an event (or state—but we need not keep adding that reminder) consists of certain conditions of that event—that is, circumstances, including both events and states of affairs, that existed just before and during the event. For example, the match bursts into flame; the conditions of this event include its having been struck a short time before, the chemicals in the match, the oxygen in the air—everything present or occurring at the time in the event's immediate environment. But some of the conditions, of course, are a good deal more relevant than others.

Let us now introduce two very important terms that we must use to talk clearly and exactly about causes: *necessary condition* and *sufficient condition*. A necessary condition of a particular event is a condition without which it would not have occurred. People can't live without oxygen, for example, so oxygen is a necessary condition of any (human) life. And when the fragile vase is knocked off the table and smashed, we may have good reason to say that if it had not been knocked off the table (at that time) it would not have broken (at that time). Now when we speak of necessary conditions of individual events, we can seldom (if ever) speak in absolute terms. It is conceivable that human lives in remote worlds are based on a very different chemistry from ours—but in *this* world, oxygen is indispensable. Again, even if the vase had not been knocked off, someone might have shot at it and smashed it. So being knocked off the table was not absolutely necessary for it to break. But under the circumstances that prevailed—no one was shooting a gun, the table was stable, and the vase was firmly placed—there would have been no breaking without the knocking off. So we can say that the knocking off was a *circumstantially necessary* condition of the vase's breaking. A circumstantially necessary condition of an event is a condition whose absence would—under the circumstances—have prevented the event from occurring.

A sufficient condition of an event is a condition under which that event *had* to happen. But single conditions are never enough to make something happen; it is always a *set* of conditions that is sufficient in this sense. Consider the vase case again: the vase was extremely fragile, the

floor was hard, the tabletop was a few feet above the floor. These conditions *plus* the knocking over would seem to be sufficient—yet we might
want to add a few more. For example, an agile fielder might have caught
the vase before it hit the floor, or might have quickly slid a cushion under
it to break the fall. So let us rule him out and add his absence to our list
of sufficient conditions. In other words, this set of conditions constitutes
the set of sufficient conditions for that particular vase's breaking:

1. the vase's being knocked over   *plus*
2. the vase's exteme fragility   *plus*
3. the floor's hardness   *plus*
4. the tabletop's being at least a few feet above the floor   *plus*
5. the absence of anyone near enough to intervene   *plus*
6. the force of gravity (of course!)

Given all these conditions, the vase *had* to break—that was inevitable.
This set of sufficient conditions is the *total cause* of the vase's breaking.

Now notice that this is not the only way to break vases; other vase
breakings might have involved different sets of sufficient conditions. So
none of the conditions in this set was absolutely necessary. Yet some or
all of them may have been circumstantially necessary conditions: given
the presence of conditions 2 to 6, the vase would not have broken without
being knocked over; given conditions 1 and 3 to 6, it would not have
broken if it had been tough instead of fragile. So the total cause of
an event includes a variety of conditions, including some that are
circumstantially necessary.

And some of these circumstantially necessary conditions are of special interest to us. If we're looking for someone to blame, we're not
interested in the nature of the floor, but in the clumsy person whose
elbow made the fatal contact—so we say it was his knocking that caused
the breaking. Here, we are using the word "cause" not for the total cause
but for an *active cause*, which is that part of the total cause that involves
an action, or at least a change, of some kind. In the same way, when
car A (in motion) makes a dent in car B (standing still), we realize that
both cars had to be there for the dent to happen. But we say that car A
caused the dent (was the active cause) because it was the car in motion.

Four mistakes are commonly made in thinking and writing about
causes.

First, it is important not to confuse necessary and sufficient conditions. There is a futile form of dispute that occasionally turns up, in
which this confusion is central.

> *A:* We cannot remedy the serious housing shortage in this country unless Congress appropriates funds to encourage building.
>
> *B:* There you go again! Can't you see that you can't automatically solve the housing problem just by another big dose of federal money?

Here, B has, of course, missed the point completely (maybe on purpose). A said that the appropriation of funds was a *necessary* condition for ending the housing shortage (in other words, the shortage could not be ended unless funds are appropriated). B replies that appropriation of funds is not *sufficient* to end the housing shortage. This is no doubt true, since the funds will have to be wisely spent, building materials will have to be available, and so on, in order for there to be sufficient conditions for ending the housing shortage. But though B claims to be refuting A, his reply is simply beside the point.

Second, we must remember that total causes (sufficient conditions) are always complex, and that active causes are only part of the story; otherwise, we will get into barren wrangling. A car goes into a skid on a turn one rainy night and crashes into someone's fence. The owner of the fence sues the driver and blames him for driving too fast: it was excessive speed, he says, that caused the accident. The driver, on the other hand, blames it all on the weather: it was the slippery road, he says, that caused the accident. Now, if they are talking about necessary conditions, they may both be right. If it hadn't been for the high speed, the accident wouldn't have happened, despite the slippery road. And if it hadn't been for the slippery road, the accident wouldn't have happened, despite the high speed. Both were part of the total cause. Neither was more or less essential than the other. So there is no point in disputing which was the "real" cause.

On the other hand, there is a point in singling out the driver's speed as the active cause in this case, and focusing special attention (and legal action) on that. For one thing, his car was in motion—unlike the road, which just lay there—and by his own act of will. For another, the road was slippery before he came on the scene; he couldn't change that, but could only change his driving to meet the dangerous road condition. So it makes sense to attach special blame to the driver—but without forgetting that his action was only part of the total cause.

Third, it is well to distinguish between immediate and remote causes of an event. What caused the flood? The dam's giving way. What caused the dam to give way? Excessive water in the reservoir. What caused the excessive water? Recent unusually high rainfall. What caused the rainfall? . . . That would involve us in meteorology, and perhaps we have gone far enough for the present. Here we have a causal chain, each link explaining the next one. What caused the flood? We can say: the dam's giving way. Or we can say: the high rainfall. For the cause of the cause of an event is a cause (but an indirect or remote cause) of that event. Of course, it would be silly to get into a dispute about whether the dam's giving way or the rainfall was the "real cause" of the flood. Both were causally involved, but as links in a chain that extended over a period of time. One was the immediate cause (the dam's giving way), the other was a more remote cause (the high rainfall).

Fourth, we can avoid the most frequent fault in causal reasoning: supposing that because one event *follows* another, it is therefore the *effect* of the other. Among the conditions that prevail when an event occurs, many will have nothing whatever to do with it. When you sneeze, a nose irritation is no doubt the active cause; but at the same time, the sun may be shining, the bees may be buzzing, and someone may be playing the piano. None of these is a circumstantially necessary condition of your sneezing; none is part of the total cause. But how often have we heard arguments such as these?

> The new sales campaign was started in March. In April, sales went up. This shows that the new sales campaign caused the rise in sales.
>
> The elementary school changed the book used in the first grade for teaching arithmetic. The pupils immediately learned faster. The new book must have caused the improvement.
>
> The Democratic mayor took office in January. Within two weeks the crime rate went down. The mayor obviously deserves great credit for making this happen.

No doubt, these are plausible causal guesses. But by themselves, the reasons are far from enough to justify accepting the proposed conclusions. All we know is that one event followed the other; but this could be a coincidence. Did the earlier event *make* the later one happen? Was it a circumstantially necessary condition—an active cause? To show that, we would have to know more about the connection between the two events. That is a question we shall come to shortly.

EXERCISE 13A

How do the distinctions made above (between circumstantially necessary and sufficient conditions, active and total cause, immediate and remote cause, causing and merely preceding) apply to the following statements?

1. The roadside restaurant's financial failure was caused by the re-routing of the highway.

2. The accident was caused by a blowout.

3. The fading of the cloth was caused by prolonged exposure to sunlight.

4. The headache was caused by eyestrain.

5. The sofa's burning was caused by its extreme flammability.

6. The boy's falling was caused by his tripping.

7. The governor's failure to win reelection was caused by his earlier efforts to institute a state income tax.

8. The death was caused by a bullet's entering the heart.

9. The death was caused by someone's pulling a trigger.

10. The plant's dying was caused by the woman's saying harsh words to it fifteen minutes earlier.

Determining the cause of a particular event (or state of affairs) is one way of explaining it. Thus, it involves the same basic logical principles that are involved in any explanation. It is a process of elimination. We think of various things that *might* have caused the event, and we try to find evidence that will eliminate all but the real cause. But to do this, we must already know what *can* cause events of that *kind*. If we are interested in a particular case—say, Uncle Henry's indigestion that occurred at 2:00 P.M. yesterday—it is important to know that overeating, ulcers, allergies, and so forth are potential causes of indigestion. So to acquire causal knowledge we must obtain some causal generalizations; that is, we must establish causal connections, not just between particular events but between *kinds* of events.

How do we establish these general causal connections? Since they are a form of generalization, the basic principles involved in establishing them are those that are involved in all generalization. We have to discover a significant association between events of one kind (scratching matches) and events of the other kind (matches bursting into flame). To say they are associated is, very roughly, to say that events of the two kinds have shown a tendency to accompany each other in our past experience. The association is significant if it is of such a nature that we are justified in expecting the association to continue in the future. A person might have been mugged four times, and each time by someone wearing a beard. In his experience, mugging and beard wearing go together. Yet the association may be of no significance, logically speaking—that is, it may give no adequate reason for believing that there is a causal connection between wearing a beard and being an active mugger (or vice versa).

To establish a causal connection, we require a number of relevant cases—that is, cases in which either the supposed cause or the supposed effect occurs, or in which both occur. And the cases should be as varied as possible; that is, the other conditions should be rather different from case to case. This shows that the causal connection we are trying to trace holds constant under various circumstances; it helps to convince us that we have found a genuine causal connection.

Assume, then, that we have a number of varied relevant cases, and that we examine them carefully to see what they tell us about possible causal connections. Suppose we find that in these cases, events of type B never occur unless they are preceded by an event of type A. Type B events might be cases of malaria; and what we find is that everyone who comes down with malaria has previously been bitten by a mosquito. This gives us a reason for concluding that being bitten by a mosquito is a necessary condition of contracting malaria.

Such general necessary conditions are a very strong form of causal connection. Once established, they permit important deductive inferences, which are conditional arguments: if we now run across someone with malaria, we can infer that he must have been bitten by a mosquito, even though neither he nor we ever saw the insect.

But remember that it takes a number and a variety of cases to establish such a necessary connection. If the cases are few, the association may be just a coincidence: like a pair of inconstant lovers, things that go together in the short run may part company in the long run. If the cases are not varied, we may overlook a hidden factor that is the real cause. Maybe there is another type of event, X, that also always precedes B—and it is really X we are after. For example, we might think it is the words of the faith healer whom Jones visits so frequently that have kept his heart problem under control—when actually it is the exercise that Jones gets in walking to the faith healer's shrine.

Suppose we find, on the other hand, that in the sample cases we have observed and studied so far, events of type A are always followed by events of type B. Every time we strike an egg sharply on the edge of the frying pan, its shell breaks. Given a number of cases under different conditions, we have reason to conclude that striking an egg in this way is part of some set of sufficient conditions for an egg's breaking. It is, in short, an active cause of egg breaking. It is not absolutely necessary, of course; there are plenty of other ways of breaking eggs. But given certain assumed conditions (the egg is a regular hen's egg, the pan is metal, the blow has some force), we can legitimately expect that future strikings of this kind will eventuate in future egg breakings. Again, we have a strong causal connection.

Now a good deal of our general causal knowledge is weaker than either of these kinds. Suppose we find that more often than not, events of type A are followed by events of type B, but this does not always happen. For example, someone invents a new drug that is designed to prevent epileptic seizures. Careful tests show that two thirds of the epileptics who take the drug stop having seizures, but one third of them are not helped. We seem to have some reason to think that the drug was effective in certain cases (it wasn't just a coincidence that those people got better), even though the association was not universal. What we have is a degree of *correlation* (not a perfect, or universal, association) between taking the drug and ending seizures. The question is: when does a correlation give us sufficient evidence of a causal connection?

This question cannot be answered except in a comparative way. The strength of the evidence rises with (1) the number of observed cases, (2) the variety of observed cases, and (3) the numerical value of the correlation. This last feature is especially important: if only fifty-two percent of our subjects get better when they take the medicine, that's not very striking, and it could be due to chance; but if eighty-five percent of them get better, it seems pretty clear that the medicine is capable of helping epileptics.

The great error in this sort of reasoning is to ignore the *negative cases*—that is, the cases from which the supposed cause is absent. Consider a very simple-minded scientist who invents a cure for the common cold. He tries it on a hundred individuals who come down with colds, and lo and behold! Nearly all of them are over their colds in five days. These results are impressive—until we ask this simple question: what would have happened if they hadn't taken the miracle drug? To answer this question, we round up a hundred other persons with colds, but we don't give them the drug—these are our negative cases—and we find that most of them, too, recover in five days. Colds generally last that long. This changes the whole picture. The logical principle is this: if those who take the drug do not show a substantially higher percentage of recovery than those who don't take the drug, then there is no evidence of a causal connection between taking the drug and recovering. One wonders whether people who claim to improve their house plants by talking nicely to them always observe this elementary precaution—of looking at a variety of negative cases.

Does poverty tend to increase criminality? Do prison sentences reduce the likelihood that criminals will commit further offenses? Does getting out on bail enable people to make a better defense when they are tried in court? Questions such as these are questions about causal connections—and very important questions they are. We cannot all be social scientists and gather the data needed to answer them; we cannot all be statisticians and subject the data to elaborate mathematical manipulation. But when we are presented with reliable data and with proposed statistical inferences from the data, we can apply basic rules of causal reasoning and escape some of the most serious logical errors.

EXERCISE 13B

Here are five arguments for a causal connection. Rate each "weak," "fair," or "strong," and give your reasons for your rating.

1. A high-school principal found that eleven percent of the seniors with an A or B average owned cars or drove them regularly; that thirty-three percent of the seniors with a C average had cars; and that sixty-two percent of the C-minus and failing students had cars. Evidently, having a car interferes with school work.

2. A study of men and women who practice transcendental meditation regularly and also drive cars shows that their accident rate is only half the national average for car drivers. This shows that transcendental meditation produces safer drivers.

3. The first time Jones ate a mango was at a neighborhood luau, a wild affair; the next morning, he developed a rash that lasted a few hours and went away. The same thing happened the next time he ate a mango, which was a wedding celebration. After that, he swore off mangoes: no use trying to beat an allergy.

4. Dr. Krankheit reported on his discovery that immunity to contagious diseases is increased by mild yoga exercises repeated several times a day. He selected as subjects a dozen men who had retired very recently (since they would be able to do the exercises without exciting adverse comment from fellow workers), and found that after beginning the exercises their susceptibility to colds and viral infections was less than half of what it had been a year earlier.

5. On three separate occasions, high winds blew down Jones's television aerial, the Wave-King. "No more Wave-King aerials for me," he resolved; "a high wind simply causes them to collapse."

EXERCISE 13C

Suppose you really want to know whether, say, Bible reading in the public schools affects student behavior, or talking to plants really improves their health. (Or select some other general causal proposition that people disagree about.) Write an essay sketching some inquiries or experiments you think ought to be undertaken to test the proposition, and explain your proposals in terms of the principles presented in this chapter.

WHAT'S TO BE DONE?

ends and means

There is a familiar and important form of reasoning that is quite different from those forms we have considered so far. It concludes not by asserting that a proposition is true, but by recommending a certain action. Consider the following arguments:

I need new batteries for my transistor radio.
Batteries can be bought at the corner drugstore.
∴ I'd better go to the drugstore.

It is right to keep a promise.
I promised to return the borrowed book.
∴ I should return the book.

It is highly desirable to halt inflation.
Inflation can be halted if we all spend less money and save more.
∴ Let's spend less and save more.

Superficially, these arguments may look like syllogisms, but they are not. They may include or depend upon some syllogistic thinking, but they are more complicated. And they wind up, not with an assertion, but with a specification of what is to be done or ought to be done. This kind of reasoning is called *practical reasoning*, because it is designed to guide action. ("Practical" is not limited here to things like fixing a bicycle—it covers everything we do; practical reasoning includes moral reasoning.) Instead of purporting to justify our belief in a proposition, practical reasoning purports to justify our decision to act in a certain way. *Practical arguments* are arguments that embody practical reasoning.

A very common form of argument to justify a decision is that which makes use of the concepts of *end* and *means*. End and means are effect and cause looked at from a practical point of view. If we know that we can produce a certain kind of effect by first producing a certain kind of cause, and if it is within our power to produce that kind of cause, then we act so as to aim at the effect—which then becomes a goal, or end, of our action. When we scratch the match, the scratching is the means by which we bring about the desired end, the match's igniting—though it may seem rather pompous to talk this way about so trivial a matter. Of course, igniting the match may be a means to a further end—say, finding a fuse-box in the dark.

An end is an event or state of affairs that is aimed at in action; it is something we intentionally try to bring about by doing something else. Thus, ends and means go together; nothing is a means unless it is used to attain an end, and nothing is an end unless some means is adopted to attain it. Both ends and means are subject to choice. We may choose which ends to aim at, and by which means to try to attain them. It is to make such decisions reasonable that we engage in practical reasoning.

To put it another way, we adopt a means *in order* to attain the end. You walk to the drugstore in order to buy the radio batteries. You return the book in order to keep a promise. You might urge others to spend less and save more in order to halt inflation. In all these cases, two elements are present, in the form of premises. First, there must be an event or state of affairs that we assume to be desirable (that is, good or valuable)—having the radio batteries, keeping a promise, stopping inflation. Second, there is a way in which we believe we can bring about this desirable end—walking to the drugstore, returning the book, saving. We must have enough knowledge of relevant causal connections to expect that the means will actually lead to the end, or will probably lead to it. Thus it makes sense to reason:

It would be desirable for the match to ignite.
∴. Let's strike it!

—since we know that striking the match (properly) will cause it to ignite. However, it would make no sense to reason:

It would be desirable for the match to ignite.
∴ Let's dip it in water!

—since we know no causal connection between being dipped in water and igniting. Moreover, we must know about our own power to adopt the contemplated means: that we are able to scratch the match, walk to the drugstore, return the book, and decrease our spending and increase our saving. Even if you would like to see some eyesore of a building reduced to rubble, and you know that this could be accomplished by a fair-sized earthquake, you are stuck at this point, unless you know a way of starting an earthquake.

The three inferences with which this chapter opened are surely legitimate, as far as they go. That is, they give a reason for concluding that such and such is the thing to do, under the circumstances. But they are not *conclusive* reasons for the decisions they lead to. They are too simple. The logical task in thinking about means and ends is always to avoid just this oversimplification, which comes from focusing attention only on particular means-ends relations, instead of viewing them in a larger living context.

There are two main, and very fundamental, errors to avoid. They can best be introduced by considering a common remark that is remarkable both for its logical insight and for its logical confusion. "The end doesn't justify the means!" How often have we heard this said in condemnation of various ways of acting that are sternly disapproved of! It is actually quite ambiguous.

The first thing to note about this remark is that it is obviously absurd. If an end doesn't justify a means, what could? Only ends can justify means—not any ends of course, but desirable ones. And this holds whether we are thinking of getting gas for a car trip, chopping down trees to make room for a supermarket, or manufacturing countless nuclear bombs. The point of using the means is to attain some end that is desired. What justifies the means is that the end is desirable—that is, worth attaining.

The second thing to note about the remark is that it contains a profound truth, which is hidden in the little word "the". *The* end never justifies a means until we have asked a further question: what other consequences will the means have? Let us grant that one effective way of defeating someone running for election is to fabricate and circulate a letter in which he is represented as making vicious remarks about various ethnic groups. But even if we assume that it is desirable to prevent him from winning, does *that* end justify *that* means? We cannot say until we have examined the other consequences that are likely to flow from using that means. The fairness of the electoral process will be undermined, someone will be unjustly treated, an illegal and immoral act will be performed, and the voters will be deprived of truths they need to know in order to make a good judgment at the polls. If we represent consequences by arrows, one hits the mark, but the others go astray:

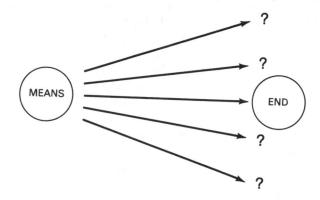

Everything we do has many consequences, some of which we can't foresee, others of which are too trival to take note of. But the first rule of good thinking about ends and means is this: before deciding to adopt a means to attain an end, consider the other consequences it is likely to have. Some of the other consequences may also be good; others may be very unfortunate. You must weigh the bad against the good, as well as you can. No single end (however good) can justify a means, then, unless the whole set of foreseeable consequences is, on balance, good.

There is a second rule of good thinking about ends and means: before deciding to adopt a means to attain an end, consider the alternative means for attaining that end. Many ends can be achieved by more than one means:

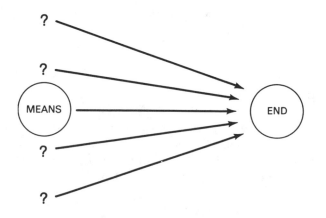

Some of these means are more efficient, more economical, more convenient, more humane, or more in accord with basic moral principles than others. There are cruel ways and kind ways—or at least crueler and less cruel ways—of slaughtering animals, of mapping out superhighways, of collecting taxes, of dealing with mental patients, and so forth. Means may be compared in countless ways, and judged to be better or worse means to a given end—though the task of weighing them may be a difficult one. Even to decide whether to take the train or drive may involve a consideration of various points. Either way, you'll arrive at the same city—the destination of your travel—but one way may be cheaper and more interesting, the other less time consuming and less tiring.

So here is another profound truth tucked away in the second "the" in the cliché about ends and means: an end, however good, does not justify *the* means until that means has been compared with alternatives available for attaining the same end. He who takes the first means that comes to mind may pay dearly (and, unfortunately, make others pay dearly, too) for his lack of logic.

It is also true, however, that there are not always alternative means to a desirable end. One might argue:

> All accused persons ought to be given a fair trial.
> No one who is denied the right to counsel can have a fair trial.
> ∴. We should make sure all accused persons have the right to counsel.

Here, the right to counsel is set forth as a necessary condition of obtaining a fair trial; if the arguer is right, then there is no way of attaining that end unless the right to counsel is conceded. That doesn't mean that we have to accept the conclusion; it does mean that we must choose between the conclusion and the major premise. In short, we have to ask what it will take to provide counsel, and whether the end is still worth it when we count the costs. ("Costs" are, of course, not limited to money; they include everything we might have to give up or forego to use that means.)

EXERCISE 14A

Here are some examples of practical reasoning. (1) What other consequences would you want to watch out for? (2) What alternative means should be considered?

1. Our children are watching the TV too much, and their schoolwork is suffering. I say let's get rid of the damn thing!

2. We'll have to tear down the Betsy Ross House. That block is the best place for the new high school.

3. The park in Rittenhouse Square is getting so messed up by the dogs that the children can't play on the grass. The thing to do is pass an ordinance to keep people from walking their dogs there.

4. What this country needs is a rigorous system of capital punishment. There is no other way of discouraging serious crimes.

5. America must become self-sufficient energy-wise within the next ten years, if our economy is to prosper. Therefore, we must begin at once to build hundreds of nuclear power plants.

We have considered some of the logical problems involved in selecting a means, once we have an end in view. But what about the end? How do we select that?

To fix on an end is to make a judgment of its worth, which is one kind of *normative judgment*. It is not enough to want the end: that will not justify the means unless the end is something that should be wanted. If you are lighting the match to cook dinner or make a fire in the fireplace, *that* means may be justified by the end—providing no untoward consequences loom ahead. If you are lighting the match to smoke a cigarette or to set fire to the schoolhouse, that end may *not* justify the means—if I may assume that these consequences, however strongly desired, are nevertheless undesirable.

How do we determine whether an end is desirable—that is, worthy of attainment? There are two preliminary principles to note before we consider normative judgments directly. First, it is always risky, sometimes disastrous, to commit yourself to an end before considering what means may be required or may be available for attaining it. You say you are determined to become a great surgeon or concert violinist, but if there is no reason to believe that you have the innate talent for that profession, the goal would be irrational to pursue. It is even more serious when people fix upon an end in a do-or-die way, and then use whatever means come to hand—even means they later regret. People have been driven to commit murder in just this way—not to mention perjury, burglary, and obstruction of justice. There may be ends worth achieving "at all costs"; but on the other hand the costs may be too great, and they should be counted before the end is finally settled on.

Second, ends themselves will often have to be judged in terms of their further consequences. Thus, to judge the desirability of the end, we may have to consider it as a means to a more distant end: the scratching of the match is a means to its igniting, its igniting is a means to lighting the oven, the lighted oven is a means to a baked cake, and so on. But in a way we have already covered this point, for among the consequences of any means are the remoter consequences of the consequences—insofar as we can foresee them.

There are two basic kinds of normative judgment that can, and must, be made of ends if those ends are to serve as logical justifications for action. The first kind consists of *appraisals of value*. We want to know how good the end is, and, more widely, whether (and how far) the total goodness of all the foreseeable consequences outweighs their total badness. There are many complexities in this problem, and we can consider only its most elementary aspects.

Appraisals of value have a typical form and are supported by a typical form of argument. Such arguments are, of course, subject to the general principles of logic that we have been considering throughout this book. But they have a feature that we have not yet considered, and it is this feature we must look at now. Here are some representative examples:

> Jones has just bought himself *a very good car.*
> Cézanne's *Card-Players* is really *a fine painting.*
> Mr. Green is *an excellent plumber.*
> This cake you just baked is [a] *first-rate* [cake].
> That was *a great party* last weekend.

(For simplicity, I consider only positive appraisals, not judgments such as "That is a lousy painting," or "This cake stinks.") We have many words of positive appraisal; all can be considered as variations on the basic one, "good." In these examples, an individual thing or person—or event—of *a certain kind* (a car, a painting, a plumber) is said to be *good of its kind—* that is, to have a certain kind of goodness to a comparatively high degree.

Each kind of thing is good (when it is good) in its own way. What makes a car good is not the same as what makes a painting or a plumber good. But something must make a car good, if it is good—it must have some properties that we expect to find, and can reasonably expect to find, in a good car. These are the properties that tend to make a car good, when it has them; they are properties that count in favor of being a good car, rather than a poor one. Thus, they can be cited in support of a favorable judgment of any particular car, for they are *criteria of car-*

goodness. For example, one criterion of car-goodness is *high mileage per gallon*. There are many others; for example:

effective brakes
speed
comfortable seats
attractive shape and color
dependability of starting in bad weather
easy handling on curves and hills

Well, you can make your own list; this one is not complete.

It may not be possible for any particular car to satisfy all the criteria of car-goodness. An engine built for high speed may not give good mileage per gallon. Still, each of these is a criterion, since they are both desirable features of cars, and so they can be reasons for preferring one car to another, or rating it higher on a scale of car-goodness. The criteria of painting-goodness may be more difficult to spell out or obtain universal agreement on, but if there are better paintings and worse ones, there must be some properties that make the better ones better and the worse ones worse. And if plumbers are not all equally good at their trade, then there must be some skills and abilities that the better ones have and the poorer ones lack.

To make a reasonable appraisal of value, then, you must ask three questions, and answer them as well as you can.

1. What kind of thing are you appraising? Anything may be of more than one kind: for instance, a man may be a plumber and a citizen. But in the context of a particular decision problem, it is generally plain what are the relevant kinds. Suppose we must decide whether to cut down a grove of trees to make way for a supermarket. Evidently we must ask, first, how good the trees are, and, second, how good a supermarket would replace them.

2. What are the criteria for that kind of thing? Of course, there may be uncertainty or difference of opinion about the answer to this question. But often, the main criteria are quite clear and uncontroversial. To decide how good a supermarket is, or will be, we apply various supermarket criteria: its size, efficiency of management, convenience, economy, accessibility to people (in the sense of saving them time and trouble), and so on. Perhaps tree criteria are not quite as plain; but we would consider their age, health, usefulness for recreation, accessibility to people (in the sense of being, perhaps, the only grove of trees in the vicinity), and so forth. There will be general agreement about many features that are desirable in, say, cars and houses and trees. In regard to plumbers, paintings, and wines, however, we may have to ask the experts in these specialized fields. If the object we are considering is of a kind that has its own specific function—as cars are designed for transportation and plumbers are trained for taking care of plumbing—the criteria depend on that function. Comfortable seats are wanted in a car so that transportation will be less effortful and tiring. And manual skills are wanted in a plumber so that he will thread the pipes properly and avoid leaks.

3. How well does the object meet the test of all the criteria? A car may be good in some respects, very good in others, poor in still others. How good a car is it? In the last analysis, you have to make a combined judgment: taken all in all, with its merits and its defects, it holds up well by the relevant criteria, and it is decidedly a good, though not great, car. Or take the painting. Considering its style, its color relationships, its subject matter, its compositional organization, its form and qualities, it is an excellent painting—perhaps the best one in the show, deserving first prize (if there are prizes). Of course, this combined judgment may be hard to make and easy to be mistaken about. So there is no call to be dogmatic. You may have to change your mind when you find out more about the car by driving it, or about the painting by living with it. Still, such judgments must be made, however tentatively, and when we can make them reasonably, we are in a position to estimate the worth of the ends we propose to attain.

The attempt to attain an end by adopting a particular means is an action—something you do, like scratching the match or buying the painting or calling the plumber. Like all actions, it is subject to the second kind of normative judgment, *moral judgment*. This kind of judgment is concerned with whether the action is right or wrong, whether it is in accord with your moral obligations or in violation of them. The philosophical problems that arise from reflection upon moral appraisal are many and deep. Yet our account of what is involved in judging ends would be seriously incomplete if we did not at least acknowledge this kind of judgment.

For here is one more hidden insight in that remark about the end not justifying the means. It may also mean that even after we have considered other consequences of adopting the means, compared the means with alternative means, and found the end to be worthwhile and worthy of pursuit, there remains another judgment to be made: would it be morally wrong to use that means? There may be means that *could* be used to attain many desirable ends, and yet for some basic ethical reason such means ought never to be used. Evidently, there are some hard questions to think about here; I can only bring them up and suggest that we all think about them, without offering to convince you of my own answers. What makes an action wrong? How can we tell when an action is wrong?

I shall not try to say. But I shall suggest one abstract principle to apply in seeking your own answers. This is the so-called principle of universalizability, and although it will not tell you what is right in every case, it will help you see what would be wrong in some cases. Actions, like objects and people, are of distinct kinds: an action may be an act of murder, of keeping a promise, of charity, of painting a picture, of installing a new hot-water heater. Its more specific kind depends on the circumstances in which it is performed: thus, it may be an act of keeping a promise about paying back money borrowed under desperate financial conditions in the honest expectation that funds would be available for repaying it in a few weeks. Now when you must make a choice about whether to act in a certain way or not, you can ask yourself this: would I be willing to have everyone act in just this way under just the circumstances I am now in? If you honestly have to reply no, you have a reason to believe that the action is wrong. If you can reply yes, you have a reason to believe that the action is not wrong. The test, in other words, is whether you can conscientiously universalize the action. To apply the test is to think of yourself simply as one person among others, treating yourself in just the same way, and by the same moral rules that you would be willing to apply to everyone else. Scratching a match to light the oven to make a cake would presumably pass this test—unless your further intention is to smuggle a file into a jail by putting it in the cake. But refusing to pay back borrowed money, even when you have the funds to do it, may not pass the test: you could not seriously wish for others to do the same to you.

At this point, we have moved beyond logic and into ethics—a rather different subject, though not unrelated. To pursue these matters would take us far afield—into equally interesting and important territory, but not that marked out for our study here. In practical reasoning, we can't draw a sharp line at the point where logical considerations shade over into ethical considerations. But surely we have passed whatever boundary there is, and so we must conclude.

One further comment is in order, though. Granted that practical reasoning is important, how does it relate to composition? It comes into play when we write not only to convince the reader that a proposition is true, but also to urge upon him a course of action. Vote for McGillicuddy! Protest the exploitation of the national forests by private lumber corporations! Write your senator today! Liberalize homosexual laws! Down with pornography! I don't picture your composition as ending with such an array of exclamation points. I merely use them to emphasize that these sentences are indeed imperatives: they are calls to action. They reflect the writer's decision, and call upon the reader for a like decision. So the arguments by which they are supported will be examples of practical reasoning. In the course of the argument, many propositions may have to be supported by nonpractical reasoning: generalizations, explanations, syllogisms, definitions, and so on. But there will also be a step at which it is decided that something is the thing to do. At this stage, the principles of reasoning about means and ends, and of making appraisals of value and moral judgments, will have to be brought to bear.

EXERCISE 14B

In each of the following decision problems, two things must be appraised. For each of them, suggest three criteria that you think would be generally agreed upon.

1. Whether to cut out funds for the department of sanitation or the city library system, in order to balance the municipal budget.

2. Whether to spend the evening working to help elect a certain political candidate or going to see a motion picture.

3. Whether to move out of the apartment and buy a house or stay where we are and use the money for a trip abroad.

4. Whether to take a bus or the subway to work.

5. Whether to choose medicine or teaching for a career.

EXERCISE 14C

Find two newspaper editorials or columns that defend roughly the same point of view regarding a current issue—that are on the same side. Let it be an issue about the proper course of action to be taken—for or against a tax reduction, the passage of a law, the building of a bridge, the firing of a public official. Write an essay showing that one of the arguments is superior to the other, when judged in terms of the principles presented in this chapter.

INDEX